D0513752

ORDER ! ORDER !

A PARLIAMENTARY MISCELLANY

ORDER ! ORDER !

A PARLIAMENTARY MISCELLANY

ROBERT ROGERS

BOOKS

First published in Great Britain in 2009 by
JR Books, 10 Greenland Street, London NW1 0ND
www.jrbooks.com

ISBN 978-1-906779-28-3

1 3 5 7 9 10 8 6 4 2

Printed by MPG Books, Bodmin, Cornwall

To Jane, Catherine and Eleanor
as always

FOREWORD

People should not do things for fun. There is no
reference to fun in any Act of Parliament.

A.P. Herbert

Despite Herbert's words, I hope that this book will provide
some fun as well as some insights and explanation about
Parliament. Each chapter has a vague theme but, in the
proper manner of a miscellany, this is quickly obscured by
entirely unconnected odds and ends. There is more about
the House of Commons than the House of Lords, but this
I attribute to the fact that I have spent 37 years at the north
end of the Palace of Westminster rather than the south end.

All anthologists owe a debt to other anthologists: those
who have, so to speak, tracked and cornered some of the
prey. That is a debt I happily acknowledge. But most of
the material in this collection comes out of a box which,
over nearly four decades at Westminster, I have been filling
with the odd, memorable, witty, historic and lunatic. (The
box is still about two-thirds full.)

I am very grateful for the help and advice of Lesley
Wilson, my editor at JR Books, and of Richard Hilliard,
an old friend and fascinated observer of Parliament. My
thanks go also to Mari Takayanagi, Archivist at the
Parliamentary Archives, and to Melanie Unwin, Deputy

Curator of Works of Art, for their expertise and enthusiasm in identifying suitable illustrations; and I am grateful for permission to reproduce those of the illustrations which are Parliamentary copyright. Thanks, too, to Richard Cracknell, Head of Social Statistics in the House of Commons Library, for his help in turning sums of money from the distant past into their modern equivalents, and to other colleagues in the Library for their assistance.

2009 has not been a good year for Parliament. For those of us whose working lives have been devoted to serving the institution and trying to make it more effective, this has been a sad time. But it may provide the basis for changes which engage the real owners of the institution – the people of the United Kingdom – more closely with their Parliament. That would be really worthwhile.

Robert Rogers

CONTENTS

I
THE PARLIAMENT
AT WESTMINSTER

That the said United Kingdom be represented by
One and the same Parliament to be stiled
The Parliament of Great Britain.
The Act of Union (1707)

⚔ PARLIAMENT ⚔

1 **The action of speaking**; a spell or bout of speaking; a speech; a talk, colloquy, conversation, conference; a discussion or debate (*obsolete*).

> *There he hulde is parlament wat were best to done.*
> (1297)

> *Thus ended the parlament betwene the fader and the sone.*
> (1450)

> *In Carbry, after a certain parliament ended betweene the*
> *Irish and English, there were taken prisoners.*
>
> (1610)

2 **A formal conference or council** for the discussion of some matter or matters of general importance; especially the name applied in the early days of the French monarchy to the assembly of the great lords of the kingdom, and in England, in the course of the 13th century, to great councils of the early Plantagenet kings.

De magno parlamento habito Londiniis in octavis Epiphaniae. ('About the great parliament held in London in the octave of the Epiphany.')

(1237)

The barons . . . to mak disturbaunce thei held a parlement. (This was the 'Mad Parliament'.)

(1330)

A noone forthe they wente; and kepte a grete perlement.

(1440)

3 **A temporary assemblage of persons**, summoned by the sovereign, and after a time dissolved.

Ces sunt les Establisemenz le Rey Edward, le fiz le Rey Henry, ez a Weymoster a son primer parlement general après son corounement. ('These are the statues of King Edward, son of King Henry, made at Westminster at his first general parliament after his coronation.')

Statute of Westminster (1275)

They were not all sturdy beggers that were in the Parlament when this lawe was stablished.

(1546)

To acquaint him [General Monk] *with their desires for a free and full Parliament.*

Samuel Pepys (1660)

4 **A permanent or continuous institution**, the composition, character and size of which have changed from time to time, but which has itself a continuous history.

These worldly prelatis that sitten in Perlement.

John Wyclif (1380)

Parliament is the highest and most honourable and absolute court of justice in England, consisting of the king, the lords of Parliament, and the Commons.

Sir Edward Coke (1628)

⊰ THE NICKNAMED PARLIAMENTS ⊱

The Addled Parliament met from 5 April to 7 June 1614, passed no Acts, and so acquired its name: no eggs hatched.

The Barebones, Little or **Nominated Parliament** of 120 Members selected by Cromwell and his Council of Officers, which sat from 4 July to 12 December 1653.

The Convention Parliament, which assembled on 25 April 1660, was so called because it was convened rather than being summoned by the king. It declared that Charles II had been the lawful monarch since the death of Charles I and set about arrangements for the Restoration.

The Devil's Parliament held by Henry VI at Coventry in 1459, which attainted the Duke of York, his son the Earl of March (afterwards Edward IV) and their followers.

The Drunken Parliament was the Scottish Parliament which met after the Restoration on 1 January 1661.

The Good Parliament, which met in 1376 and sought to end various abuses.

The Lack-Learning, Unlearned or **Dunces Parliament**, which met at Coventry in 1404 in obedience to Henry IV's summons which stipulated that *no lawyers should be returned as Members.*

The Short Parliament sat from 13 April to 5 May 1640 and was succeeded by the Long Parliament.

The Long Parliament, which first met on 3 November 1640, began the Civil War, put Charles I on trial and ensured that he was condemned to death, was 'purged' by Colonel Pride and the Republicans in 1648, was sent packing by Cromwell in 1653 and restored in 1659, and was finally dissolved in March 1660 after restoring Charles II.

The Mad Parliament (*parlamentum insanum*) consisted of the barons who met at Oxford in 1258.

The Marvellous, Wonderful or **Wonder-Working Parliament** (also known as the Merciless or Unmerciful Parliament, depending which side you were on) of 1388, which condemned the favourites of Richard II.

The Model Parliament summoned by Edward I in 1295 was the first to include representatives of the shires, cities and boroughs as well as the clergy and aristocracy.

The Pensioner or **Cavalier Parliament** was the first Parliament of Charles II and sat from 1661 to 1679 (it was also known as his Long Parliament).

The Running Parliament was used of the Scottish Parliament, from its sittings being moved from place to place.

The Rump Parliament was the name given to the 1640 Long Parliament in the last part of its 20-year life.

The Unreported Parliament sat from 10 May 1768 to 13 June 1774 and is so called from a gap in the reports of parliamentary debates.

The Useless Parliament was the first Parliament of Charles I, which sat from 18 June to 12 August 1625.

❧ SOME PARLIAMENT THINGS ☙

A parliament **cake**: a thin crisp gingerbread biscuit.

A parliament **Christmas**: a grudging name for the lack of a Christmas holiday under the Puritan Long Parliament during the Commonwealth 1649–1660.

A parliament **clock**: also called an Act of Parliament clock, this was a clock put up following the introduction of a clock tax in 1797. The annual rate varied from two shillings and sixpence – half a crown, or 12½p – up to 10 shillings (50p) for a gold watch. People stopped buying clocks and watches, with predictable results for the trade. Businesses and public institutions put up parliament clocks that the public could see; but the tax was repealed after a year.

A parliament **heel**: to heel a ship over a few degrees in order to be able to repair or clean the hull more easily. The *Royal George*, Admiral Kempenfelt's flagship, was supposed to be given only a 'parliament heel' when anchored off Spithead on 29 August 1782 (in this case to repair a leak below the waterline). The starboard guns were shifted to port, a loud crack was heard, and the ship went down, with the Admiral and 800 men. The event was commemorated by William Cowper in a truly dreadful piece of verse:

Toll for the brave
The brave that are no more
All sunk beneath the wave
Fast by their native shore

Eight hundred of the brave
Whose courage was well tried
Had made the vessel heel
And laid her on her side

A land breeze shook the shroud[1]
And she was overset
Down went the Royal George
With all her crew complete

Lady Austen had asked Cowper to write something that would fit the tune of Handel's March from *Scipio*, and Cowper claimed afterwards that he had had great difficulty in fitting the words to the music. Not the only difficulty, then.

A parliament **hinge**: a hinge that projects from the wall, so that a door or window, when opened, can swing back flush against the wall.

[1] Not only inaccurate (the Court of Inquiry found that the problem was a structural one in the hull) but not very seamanlike: the shrouds in a ship of the line were solid pieces of standing rigging. A land breeze which shook the shrouds that much would probably have demolished a few houses in Portsmouth.

⊰ STRANGERS ⊱

'Strangers' is the term used for centuries for **visitors to Parliament**. Thus, Strangers' Gallery and Strangers' Bar. In 2004 the House of Commons agreed to a proposal by a select committee to drop the term in favour of the less dismissive 'visitors'. Some debate arose about how to handle the scene in the Central Lobby each day as the Speaker's procession passes through on the way to prayers and the police inspector on duty calls out *Hats off, Strangers*. The late Eric Forth, Member for Bromley and Chislehurst, suggested that a suitably modern alternative would be *Hats off, Stakeholders*; but this is one use of 'Strangers' that has survived unchanged.

⊰ ECHOES OF THE PAST ⊱

At the end of every sitting of the House of Commons the policemen and doorkeepers shout *Who goes home?* (usually abbreviated to a long, drawn out 'Ho-o-o-o-ome'). This is a survival from the days when MPs on their way home would band together as a defence against highway-men and footpads.

When an MP presents a Ten-Minute Rule Bill, or when a senior Whip delivers an answer from the Queen to an Address from the House of Commons, he or she bows at the Bar of the House, advances up the floor, bows half-way and then bows again at the Table. The halfway bow is where, in the old Chamber destroyed by fire in 1834, MPs would bow under the great chandelier lost in the fire. It was known then as 'bowing at the branch'.

When the bewigged Clerks at the Table write in the *Minute Book* of the House, they use abbreviations that would have been familiar to their predecessors three centuries ago: 'Question proposed' (in other words, when the Chair tells the House what is to be decided) is *Qn ppd.* A Bill 'Read the first time; ordered to be read a second time tomorrow and to be printed' is *Read 1º; to be read 2º tw P.* 'To lie upon the Table' (when the House is in possession of a paper but no immediate action is to be taken) is simply *T.*

Erskine May's Treatise on the Law, Privileges, Proceedings and Usage of Parliament is the single authoritative work on parliamentary practice. **Sir Thomas Erskine May** (later Lord Farnborough), Clerk of the House from 1871 to 1886, wrote the first nine editions himself, and subsequent editions (the current one is the 23rd) have been edited by the Clerk of the House of the day.

When May was looking for a way of justifying Speaker Brand's somewhat high-handed introduction of the closure in 1881 (see page 89), he came across a helpful case in 1604, and said: '*I have found what convinces the House more readily than any argument. I have found a precedent.*'

When Brand retired as Speaker he wrote to his successor, Arthur Wellesley Peel: '*my advice to you will be trust May and the House.*'

John Hatsell, Clerk of the House from 1768 to 1820 (but only nominally from 1797 onwards) wrote *Precedents of Proceedings*, which remained influential even after May's work appeared (and is still consulted today). He summed up the need for parliamentary rules:

> *It is more material that there should be a rule to go by than what that rule is; in order that there may be a uniformity of proceeding in the business of the House, not subject to the momentary caprice of the Speaker or to the captious disputes of any of the Members.*

John Hatsell, Clerk of the House of Commons from 1768 to 1820

⊰ EPITAPH ON A SPEAKER ⊱

The epitaph of **Thomas Williams**, Speaker 1563, at Harford Church, Ivybridge, Devon:

Here lyeth the corps of Thomas Williams esquire
Twice reader he in court appointed was,
Whose sacred minde to vertu did aspire
Of Parlament he Speaker hence did passe

The comen peace he studied to preserve
And trew relygion ever to maintayne
And now in heaven with mightie Jove doth Raigne

⊰ FIRST IMPRESSIONS ⊱

Parliament meets in the old King's Palace. St Stephen's Chapel, formerly the Royal Chapel of the Palace, but lately beautified for the convenience of the House of Commons, was a very indifferent place, old and decayed.

Daniel Defoe *A Tour through the Whole Island of Great Britain* (1724)

The House of Commons is plainly and neatly fitted up, and accommodated with galleries, supported by slender iron pillars, adorned with Corinthian capitals and sconces. At the upper end, the Speaker is placed upon a raised seat. Before him is the Table, at which the Clerk and his assistants sit. Just below the Chair, and on each side, the Members seat themselves. The Speaker and Clerks always wear gowns in the House.

Thomas Pyne *The Microcosm of London* (1808)

The House of Commons is like a church. The vaulted roofs and stained glass windows, the rows of statues of great statesmen of the past, the echoing halls, the soft-footed attendants and the whispered conversations, contrast depressingly with the crowded meetings and the clash and clang of hot opinions he has just left behind in the election campaign. Here he is, a tribune of the people, coming to make his voice heard in the seats of power. Instead, it seems that he is expected to worship; and the most conservative of all religions: ancestor worship.

Aneurin Bevan *In Place of Fear* (1952)

Through the eyes of an American visitor:

Beyond the hall lay a circular chamber with passages leading out of it in various directions, rows of telephone boxes on one side and a polished counter on the other. It struck me as being incredibly like the entrance hall of a second-rate hotel.

Dorothy Jane Ward *English Enigma* (1948)

Ladies arriving at Members' Entrance for tea, 1893

⚜ VISITING THE HOUSES OF PARLIAMENT ⚜

Stephen Leacock, Canadian humorist (and Professor of Political Economy at McGill University), writing in 1922:

The public are no longer allowed restricted access to the Houses of Parliament; its approaches are now strictly guarded by policemen. In order to obtain admission it is necessary (A) to communicate in writing with the Speaker of the House, enclosing certificates of naturalisation and proof of identity or (B) give the policeman five shillings. Method B is the one usually adopted. On great nights, however, when the House of Commons is about to do something important, such as ratifying a Home Rule Bill, or cheering, or welcoming a new lady Member, it is not possible to enter by merely bribing the policeman with five shillings; it takes a pound. The English people complain bitterly of the rich Americans who have in this way corrupted the London public. Before they were corrupted they would do anything for sixpence.

My Discovery of England

In 2008 there were **984,560 visitors** to the Houses of Parliament, an increase on 2006 (890,460) and 2007 (962,410). 111,310 visited the Gallery of the House of Commons, while 67,350 visited the Gallery of the House of Lords.

Education Service visits, providing schools with an experience of Parliament, have increased dramatically: 2006: 10,970 pupils; 2007: 24,140; and 2008: 33,390.

◄ PARLIAMENTARY TIMES ►

A Parliament: the period between the summoning of a new Parliament and its dissolution. The average length since 1945 has been three years and seven months, but four years is about the modern norm.

A session: the period between the State Opening of Parliament and Prorogation, usually from November to November; but the first session of a new Parliament is 18 months if the general election is in the spring or early summer.

Prorogation: both the ending of a session (by the sovereign), and the period from then until the State Opening and the start of a new session. This period is the only one properly called a recess, although periods of adjournment are also generally called recesses.

A sitting: the day's business from prayers (see Epilogue, page 242) to the adjournment. The average length of House of Commons sittings in 2008–09 was 7 hours 37 minutes.

An adjournment: 1. the end of a sitting; 2. the proper name for a recess (the non-sitting times at Christmas, Easter, Whitsun and in the late summer).

◄ THE PARLIAMENTARY ARCHIVES ►

The Archives in the Victoria Tower occupy 12 floors, have five-and-a-half miles (almost 9 kilometres) of shelving, and hold about three million documents.

To preserve the records, they are kept at a constant 16°C and 55% relative humidity, with pollution filters.

The Archives contain the original copies of 64,000 Acts of Parliament from 1497 and the manuscript *Journals* of the House of Lords from 1510 and the House of Commons from 1547. Almost all the other original records of the House of Commons were lost in the fire of 1834.

◄ THE MAXIMUM LIFE OF A PARLIAMENT ►

A parliament's lifespan cannot exceed five years, from first meeting to dissolution. From the Septennial Act 1715 to the Parliament Act 1911 the period was seven years.

During the First World War the 1911 Parliament was extended to eight years by the Parliament and Registration Act 1916 and the Parliament and Local Elections Act 1918.

During the Second World War the 1935 Parliament was extended by the Prolongation of Parliament Acts 1940, 1941, 1942, 1943 and 1944.

⊰ ANIMALS IN PARLIAMENT ⊱

In times past the informality of Westminster allowed casual and unregulated access to Parliament, both by passers-by and, no doubt, by **animals**. We may be sure that the 'spanyell' recorded in the *Journal* of 1606 as wandering into the Chamber was not unusual (see page 64).

In the 21st century things are very different. But there is more **livestock** in the Palace, with or without permission, than one might imagine.

Metropolitan Police **dogs** trained to sniff explosives are a daily sight at Westminster; so too have been David Blunkett's guide dogs Lucy, Ted and Offa, and the present incumbent, Sadie.

In the House of Commons part of the Parliamentary Estate there were 200 sightings of **mice** in 2001; but these had fallen to 81 in 2007. In May 2008 the peak of an infestation by the common house **moth** (*Tineola bisselliella*) was reached with a moth count of 2,507; in 2008 this had fallen to 907.

On the roof of the Palace less destructive moths can be spotted, attracted by the powerful floodlights. In a recent count 200 different species were identified – an extraordinary number for urban Westminster – and perhaps a factor in attracting the bats – both pipistrelle (*Pipistrellus pipistrellus*) and noctule (*Nyctalus noctula*).

A professional falconer is retained by the Parliamentary Estates Directorate; his **Harris hawks** discourage the pigeons that scavenge for food, and the seagulls which are ready to steal from unfortunate lunchers on the Terrace – to say nothing of their (the birds') generous droppings.

But the most elegant wild creatures at Westminster are the **peregrine falcons** (*Falco peregrinus*) which nest on the Victoria Tower, and are provided with a nestbox jointly by the parliamentary authorities and by Natural England.

⊰ LORDS AND COMMONS CRICKET ⊱

The **Lords and Commons Cricket Club**, founded in 1850, is one of the older cricket clubs in the world, and has some of the oldest club colours (blue and gold). Members, officers and staff of both Houses are eligible to play; but there is also a fine tradition of 'ringers' dating back to the club's foundation.

Probably the **first Lords and Commons match** was that against I Zingari at Vincent Square, Westminster, on 22 June 1850. Lords and Commons scored 75 in their first innings; IZ 97; and the match was unfinished after Lords and Commons had scored 132 in their second innings. On this occasion the ringer was John Wisden, the founder of *Wisden's Cricketers' Almanac*, and at the time one of the best bowlers in the country. He was a shrewd choice; he was second top scorer in the Lords and Commons first innings, and then took nine IZ wickets (the tenth was a run-out).

Three captains of England have also been **captains of Lords and Commons**: Lord Harris, who first captained England in 1879 and captained Lords and Commons in the 1920s; Sir Stanley Jackson, who captained England against the Australians in 1905 and also played for Lords and Commons in the 1920s; and the Honourable Lionel (later Lord) Tennyson, who captained Hampshire from 1919 to 1933, and England in the 1921 series against the Australians. It is probable that Lord Hawke, who captained Yorkshire from 1883 to 1910 and England in four tests in South Africa, also played for Lords and Commons; but the scorebooks which would confirm this are no more.

Brian Johnston, the commentator who for many was the voice of cricket, kept wicket for Lords and Commons in June 1933, at the invitation of Lord Dunglass MP, better known later as Sir Alec Douglas-Home (Oxford, MCC and

Middlesex). He had two stumpings off the slow leg-breaks of Lord Ebbisham, later recounting:

> *Lord Ebbisham was so slow that in one match he appealed against a batsman who was plumb l.b.w. 'Not out,' said the umpire. It looked so obviously out that even his Lordship could not resist a tiny bit of dissent. 'Why not?' he queried politely. 'Because,' replied the umpire, 'the ball was going so slowly it would never have reached the stumps!'*

Sir Alec Douglas-Home, by the way, is the only British Prime Minister to have played first-class cricket, although the game still has a lifelong supporter and enthusiast in Sir John Major.

> *My wife had an uncle who could never walk down the nave of Westminster Abbey without wondering whether it would take spin.*
>
> Sir Alec Douglas-Home

When Foreign Secretary, Douglas-Home was not known for his appetite for paperwork. In his red ministerial box one weekend his Private Office put a vast report on the Icelandic fishing industry with a note: *The Foreign Secretary may care to read this over the weekend.* When the box came back on Monday, added to the note were the words: *A kindly thought, but erroneous.*

⊰ PARLIAMENT ON THE AIR ⊱

The BBC first asked permission to broadcast Parliament in 1923, when it wanted to broadcast the King's Speech at the State Opening in that year. It did not have that many parliamentary friends:

> *Not only in private conversation but in every newspaper the utmost indignation is manifested against the Corporation . . . The Corporation is dismally failing. I prognosticated at the time it was instituted that it was bound to fail.*

Leslie Hore-Belisha (1928)

Nor was there much support for editorial freedom:

> *It cannot be doubted that transmission by broadcast is now one of the most potent political forces in the world and if political issues are to be selected for the country we believe that they ought to be selected in the House of Commons and not at Broadcasting House . . . Obviously if matters for debate over the broadcast are selected by the British Broadcasting Corporation, there is a danger that they may create issues which perfectly justly they may think are the major political issues at the moment but in regard to which Members of this House would not agree.*

Sir Stafford Cripps (1933)

Perhaps surprisingly for one who was so effective an orator in the House of Commons, **Churchill** was strongly opposed to the broadcasting of proceedings:

> *On the whole it will be found to be in the long interests of the House of Commons to observe the practice which has been observed for a considerable time . . .*

(1955)

He was supported by **Clement Attlee**, who was worried about the appearance of the broadcasting 'personality':

> *I do not quite know how the people who appear on the wireless are selected. I am told that the selection is based on their entertainment value.*

(1955)

Regular **sound broadcasting** of both Houses and their committees began on 3 April 1978.

Televising of the House of Lords began on 23 January 1985.

Televising of the House of Commons began on 21 November 1989, having been rejected in 1966, 1971, 1975 and 1985. Even when it was approved, the majority – 320 in favour and 266 against – was hardly overwhelming.

In a debate in 1991 on the experience of televising the House, the Labour MP Tony Banks said:

> *There have not been the rows and scenes of hooliganism that the Jonahs were foretelling. No-one has done a runner with the Mace since televising began – although it happened twice before. No-one has attempted to pull off Mr Speaker's wig in an attempt to get a bit of cheap publicity. There have been no streakers and we have had very little crowd violence. Indeed, behaviour in the place has improved since televising began. That is not because honourable Members are conscious of the cameras, but because behaviour in this place is fairly good in comparison with legislatures around the world.*
>
> Hansard (1 May 1991)

Sir Humphrey Appleby and Bernard Woolley in the TV series *Yes, Minister*:

Sir Humphrey:	*Ministers should never know more than they need to know. Then they can't tell anyone. Like secret agents, they could be captured and tortured.*
Bernard Woolley:	*You mean by terrorists?*
Sir Humphrey:	*By the BBC.*

⇥ THE PRESS ⇤

Robert Cecil, Marquess of Salisbury, about the *Daily Mail*:
> *By office boys for office boys.*

The 10th Duke of Devonshire, on hearing of an attack by Stanley Baldwin on newspaper proprietors:
> *Good God! That's done it. He's lost us the tarts' vote.*

⇥ NOUNS OF NUMBER ⇤

Nouns of number or multitude, such as Mob, Parliament, Rabble, House of Commons, Regiment, Court of King's Bench, Den of Thieves, and the like.
William Cobbett, *Grammar of the English Language*, letter xvii: Syntax as Relating to Pronouns (1824)

⇥ THE OLD CHESTNUTS ⇤

There are many **stories** told about Parliament that have passed into the folklore. For the purpose of telling they usually have names attached to them, but this makes them no less apocryphal.

The peer who dreamed that he was making a speech in the House of Lords . . . and woke up to find that he was.

The extraordinarily loquacious House of Commons barber (in the barber's shop deep in the bowels of the building) was feared by those unable to cope with his flood of reminiscence and rhetorical questions. Asked how his client of the moment would like his hair cut, the barber received the reply: *In silence, please*. This story is told of Quintin Hogg, Enoch Powell and many others, including Churchill himself.

Rather more plausibly, **Churchill** is supposed to have said when asked the same question: *A man of my limited resources cannot presume to have a hair style. Get on and cut it.*

A senior member of the Cabinet was walking through a crowded Central Lobby one day. Seeing a friend in the distance, he shouted '*Neil!*' Two hundred tourists obediently sank to their knees.

An MP who finds it difficult to say anything quickly, or pithily, or wittily has bored an audience for much longer than they had any right to expect. Suddenly realising that she is about to get the bird, she says: *I'm so sorry. I've gone on for much too long. My only excuse is that there isn't a single clock in the room.* Morose voice from the back: *No, but there's a calendar behind you.*

An overworked and overwrought MP is getting grief from his wife who is fed up with seeing him only at weekends, and then only in the gaps between constituency surgeries and civic events. *You don't really care about me,* she says, *so what would you do if you found me in bed with another man?* The MP has had enough: *Shoot his guide dog.*

⊸ AND THE FICTIONAL HISTORY ⊱

Ingenious and picturesque explanations for things are part of all **folklore**. But beware if your guide around the Houses of Parliament tells you any of the following . . .

The Petition Bag on the back of the Speaker's Chair is the origin of the phrase 'It's in the bag'. Nonsense. Not until your rabbit or pheasant was 'in the bag' could you count upon it. It's a phrase much older than the Petition Bag.

The Petition Bag, in which a petition is placed when it has been presented by an MP

The lines on the floor of the Commons Chamber are two sword-lengths apart and – because MPs may not step over the lines when speaking – were designed to prevent them running each other through. Not likely. One, there's never been a time on record when Members were allowed to bring swords into the Chamber (indeed, the loops of pink ribbon in the Members' Cloakroom are a survival from the time when that was where they parked their swords); two, if an MP of an earlier age were to be so outraged with an opponent as to be setting about him with cold steel, it is unlikely that a line on the carpet would stop him; and three, there were no lines on the floor of the Chamber in the days when gentlemen carried swords.

MPs turn and face the benches during prayers because it was then easier to kneel when wearing a sword. No. Not only is there the sword problem (see above) but even without a sword it's well-nigh impossible to kneel when facing the other way.

The expression 'toe the line' comes from the lines on the Commons Chamber floor. Nonsense. The expression comes from the Royal Navy of Nelson's time and before, when seamen were assembled for inspection by divisions, and lined up with their bare feet on seams in the deck planking.

The Westminster Parliament is the 'Mother of Parliaments'. Fair enough given that the transition from Empire to Commonwealth spread the Westminster system around the world (and it is worth remembering that some of the leading figures in the early days of the American colonies had Westminster experience). But strictly speaking this is a misquotation. It was England that John Bright in 1865 described as the 'Mother of Parliaments'. Bright (1811–1889), MP for Manchester 1843–1857, lost that seat for his opposition to the Crimean War. He quickly became one of Birmingham's two MPs, serving in Parliament for a further 30 years.

⚜ COMMERCIAL OPPORTUNITIES ⚜

A letter to *The Times* from **Lord Rosebery** (Prime Minister 1894–1895):

Sir,
Will you assist an embarrassed old fogey to understand the present position, for he hears that in the newspapers it is reported that negotiations are going on with regard to a certain electoral fund, in the possession of Mr Lloyd George, which appears to be a main asset in the business.

Now the question, which is never asked, but which must occur to us all, is: What is this sum, how was it obtained and what is its source? Certainly it is not from Mr Lloyd George's private means; it comes from some other direction. What is this? It surely cannot be the sale of the Royal Honours. If that were so, there would be nothing in the worst times of Charles II or Sir Robert Walpole to equal it. But what amazes me is this: no one seems to think that there would be anything unusual in such a sale. If so, all the worse, for it would be the prostitution of the Royal Prerogative, and so the ruin of the British Constitution.

On such a matter there should be no possibility of doubt. Scores, nay hundreds of 'Honours' have been distributed. Have any been sold and helped to produce the sum in question? An authoritative statement should be furnished as to the source of this fund.

I am, Sir, yours respectfully,
ROSEBERY
February 16th, 1927

Lloyd George, Prime Minister from 1916 to 1922, said in 1920 that he regarded the sale of titles as *the cleanest way of raising money for a political party*. As an agent he employed Maundy Gregory, a repellent fixer (and, rather oddly, the son of a vicar). Maundy Gregory had a price list, and the prices were high: £80,000 to £120,000 for a viscountcy and £10,000 to £15,000 for a knighthood. The present anthologist's great-grandfather was offered a baronetcy (not, he hastens to add, by Maundy Gregory but by Lloyd George himself); but, being a Welshman just as canny as Lloyd George, decided that the price was exorbitant for all the good it would do him.

One purchaser of a peerage took the crafty precaution of opening a bank account in the name of the title he had chosen, and then writing a cheque for the fee on that account. In order to cash the cheque, Maundy Gregory (and Lloyd George) had to deliver.

Another client paid over £30,000 but then died before the honour could be delivered. His executors were quick to ask for the money back. Gregory initially refused, but paid up in three instalments when they threatened to sue.

The trade in honours caused remarkably little comment in the press. This was ascribed mainly to newspaper proprietors benefiting from special offers on titles.

'The Fountain of Honour', from Truth *magazine, 1912*

After Lloyd George left Number 10, political pressure resulted in a Royal Commission, which in turn led to the Honours (Prevention of Abuses) Act 1925. But it was only Maundy Gregory who got caught by it when he continued the trade on the basis of private enterprise. He served two months and left for France (with, it was widely thought, a substantial proportion of the takings, and just ahead of inquiries into the suspicious death of his friend Mrs Edith Rosse), never to return.

Around that time Horatio Bottomley, one of only three MPs expelled from the House in the 20th century, was serving a prison sentence, having been convicted of fraud in 1922. When a friend visited him in prison, he was surrounded by mailbags. *Sewing?*, asked the friend. *No*, said Bottomley. *Reaping*.

Bottomley congratulated F.E. Smith (1872–1930) on becoming Lord Chancellor and said: *In fact, F.E., I wouldn't have been surprised to hear that you had been made Archbishop of Canterbury.*

In that case, said Smith, *I should certainly have asked you to come to my enthronement.*

That's very good of you, said Bottomley.

Not at all, said Smith. *I should have needed a crook.*

George Bernard Shaw once said: *I've been offered titles, but I think they get one into disreputable company.*

⚜ FROM *DR JOHNSON'S DICTIONARY* ⚜

debate: A personal dispute; a controversy. A quarrel; a contest.

to debate: To controvert; to dispute; to deliberate; to engage in combat.

debater: A disputant; a controvertist.

Parliament: The assembly of the King and the three estates of the realm, namely the lords spiritual, the lords temporal, and commons, for the debating of matters touching the commonwealth, especially the making and correcting of laws; which assembly or court is, of all the others, the highest.

politically; Artfully; cunningly.

politician: One versed in the arts of government; one skilled in politics. A man of artifice; one of deep contrivance.

II

THE GREAT PALACE

This little room is the shrine of the world's liberties.
Winston Churchill

The oldest part of the Palace is Westminster Hall, whose walls date from 1097. Its floor area is nearly 1,550 square metres (1,850 square yards). The Hall was magnificently rebuilt in the reign of Richard II (1377–1399). The Clerk of the Works for two years in the early stages of the rebuilding was a young man named . . . Geoffrey Chaucer.

Trials in the Hall have included those of Sir William Wallace (1305), Sir Thomas More (1535), Guy Fawkes and the Gunpowder Plot conspirators (1606), Charles I (1649), the rebel lords of the 1715 rebellion (1716), the rebel lords of the 1745 rebellion (1746–1747) and Warren Hastings (1788–1795).

Amongst Lyings-in-State in the Hall have been those of William Ewart Gladstone (1898), Edward VII (1910), George V (1936), George VI (1952), Queen Mary (1953),

Sir Winston Churchill (1965) and Queen Elizabeth the Queen Mother in 2002.

The old Parliament buildings around the Hall, though picturesque, were stuffy, smelly and cramped:

> *. . . notoriously imperfect, very crazy as buildings, and extremely incommodious in their local distribution. I know of no advantage whatever that attends the present adjacent accommodation or the accesses to the House. They are not well disposed for the transaction of business; they are not symmetrical with the House of Lords; they are not symmetrical with Westminster Hall; there is no proper access for Members, although we have the misfortune to see the Prime Minister . . . murdered in the Lobby; and, on several occasions, Members have been personally insulted in going to the House. A Member who does his duty in Parliament is sometimes liable to offend individuals; he must pass every day of his life up a series of narrow, dark, tortuous passages, where any individual who wishes to insult him may have the certain and easy opportunity of doing so.*

John Wilson Croker MP (1833)

⊣ THE FIRE ⊢

A cure for Croker's complaints was not long in coming: on 16 October 1834 most of the medieval buildings of the old

Palace burned down; the fire started through the over-enthusiastic stoking of the furnaces beneath the House of Lords with tally sticks (hazel sticks on which the amount of tax due from an individual was recorded; the stick could be split to provide a demand and a bill – or receipt).

The Office of Works report on the fire read, somewhat repetitively:

> *The Painted Chamber, totally destroyed. The House, libraries, committee-rooms, housekeeper's rooms, &c, are totally destroyed (in the Commons); the official residence of Mr Ley (the Clerk of the House of Commons) – this building is totally destroyed. All the rooms from the oriel window to the south side of the House of Commons are totally destroyed. Westminster Hall: no damage has been done to this building.*

The Destruction of the Houses of Lords and Commons by Fire, 16 October 1834

◄ THE NEW PALACE OF WESTMINSTER ►

The competition to design the new Palace had 97 entries, identified only by a motto or pseudonym. The winner was Sir Charles Barry, entry number 64. He estimated that building the new Palace would take six years and cost £724,986. It took 30 years and cost three times that amount.

The House of Lords first sat in their Chamber in 1847, and the House of Commons first sat in theirs in 1850 (but did not move in permanently for another two years).

Barry's House of Lords (with details and embellishment – as throughout the Palace – by Augustus Welby Pugin) was grand. By contrast the Commons Chamber was plain and indeed intimate:

> *Churchill called me into the Chamber to take a last look around. All was darkness except for a faint light around under the Gallery. We could dimly see the Table but walls and roof were invisible. 'Look at it,' he said. 'This little place is what makes the difference between us and Germany. It is in virtue of this that we shall muddle through to success and for lack of this Germany's brilliant efficiency leads her to destruction. This little room is the shrine of the world's liberties.'*
> Diary of Alexander McCallum Scott (March 1917)

The Palace of Westminster has:

3,142 offices (including 984 offices for Members of both Houses)

1,531 corridors

876 stairways

812 plant rooms

530 lavatories

91 meeting rooms

22 passenger lifts

The Palace is only one of the buildings on the Parliamentary Estate; there are parliamentary offices in a further 15 buildings in London SW1.

Stephen Leacock again:

. . . for the ordinary visitor to London the greatest interest attaches to the Parliament buildings. The House of Commons is commodiously situated beside the River Thames: the principal features of the House are the large lunch-room on the western side and the tea-room on the eastern. A series of smaller luncheon-rooms extend (apparently) all round about the premises; while a commodious bar offers a ready access to the Members at all hours of the day. While any Members are in the bar a light is kept burning in the tall Clock Tower at one corner of the building, but when the bar is closed the light is turned off, by whichever of the Scotch Members leaves last.

There is a handsome legislative chamber attached to the premises from which – so the antiquarians tell us –

the House of Commons took its name. But it is not usual now for the Members to sit in the legislative chamber as the legislation is now all done outside, either at the home of Mr Lloyd George or at the National Liberal Club, or at one or other of the newspaper offices.

The House, however, is called together at very frequent intervals to give it the opportunity of hearing the latest legislation and allowing the Members to indulge in cheers, sighs, groans, votes, and other expressions of vitality. After having cheered as much as is good for them, they go back again to the lunch-rooms and go on eating until they are needed again.

My Discovery of England, 1922

⊰ A GERMAN ADMIRER ⊱

When Kenneth Mackenzie, later Clerk of Public Bills (and incidentally a renowned translator of works in Latin, Greek and Polish), was preparing a revised edition of his guide to the House of Commons, he included a laudatory quotation about 'Barry's masterpiece, its thousand windows reflected in the waters of the River Thames', and gave its author. The quotation was fine; the author was not; it was Adolf Hitler, and it came from *Mein Kampf*. James Callaghan, then a new MP, complained to the Speaker, and the Speaker instructed that a piece of paper should be stuck over the offending words.

Sir Barnett Cocks, the Clerk of the House of Commons from 1963 to 1972, described how the words still showed faintly through the paper, 'intriguing by their very obscurity. Finally it was decided to destroy all copies other than those already sold, which subsequently became treasured collectors' items.'

⊰ THE CLOCK TOWER AND BIG BEN ⊱

You should never confuse the two. Big Ben is the hour bell of the Great Clock of Westminster, and the Clock Tower is where it is housed.

The Clock Tower is 314 feet (96 metres) high and 40 feet (12.1 metres) square. There are 393 steps to the lantern room (through 11 floors) but visitors to the clock platform have to climb (only) 334 steps. The Clock Tower contains 30,000 cubic feet (850 cubic metres) of stone and 92,000 cubic feet (2,600 cubic metres) of bricks.

The Tower actually stands on the site of a much older clock tower, built by Henry Yvele, the architect of Westminster Hall, in 1365. That tower was demolished around 1698 under the direction of Sir Christopher Wren, rather better known for putting things up than pulling them down.

Big Ben's predecessor, the bell of the old clock tower, was known as 'Edward of Westminster'. When Wren pulled down the old tower, Edward of Westminster was sold for £385.17s.6d, taken to St Paul's Cathedral, then being built under the direction of . . . er . . . Sir Christopher Wren, and now hangs in the north-west tower of the Cathedral.

Big Ben, the hour bell of the Great Clock, was cast at the Warner Foundry in Stockton-on-Tees and brought to London by sea in October 1856. It then weighed more than 16½ tons, and was transported to the Clock Tower, through cheering crowds, on a trolley drawn by 16 horses.

But a year later a four-foot crack was discovered, and the bell had to be recast at the Whitechapel Bell Foundry. In the process it lost three tons. It was rehung in October 1858 (it took 18 hours to pull the bell 200 feet – 60 metres – up to the belfry); it was turned so that a different part was struck, and the weight of the hammer was reduced to 440 pounds (200 kilograms). The original hammer is kept at the House.

The chimes of Big Ben were first broadcast at midnight on 31 December 1923.

Why 'Big Ben'? Possibly after Sir Benjamin Hall, who was first Commissioner of Works when it was hung. But more probably after Benjamin Caunt, the bare-knuckle prize fighter. He fought his last fight in 1857; he weighed 17 stone (108 kilograms) and fought 60 rounds for a draw. He was 42 years old.

The Great Clock was the answer to the call from the Office of Works for:

> *A noble clock, indeed the king of clocks, the biggest the world has ever seen, within sight and sound of the throbbing heart of London.*

It was designed by Professor George Airey, the Astronomer Royal, and a polymath QC, Edmund Denison, who was an inventor of all sorts of things but especially unhinged on the subject of clocks. He later became Lord Grimthorpe, and the mechanism of the Great Clock is the 'Grimthorpe double three-legged gravity'. Up to then, for any outdoor clock, the wind blowing on the clock hands slowed the mechanism. The Grimthorpe double three-legged gravity solved the problem, and became a standard mechanism for public clocks.

The Great Clock was started on 31 May 1859.

The dials are each 23 feet (7 metres) across.

There are 312 pieces of **glass** in each face. They are lit by 28 (energy-efficient!) **bulbs** of 85 watts each, which have a life of 60,000 hours.

The figures are two feet (61 cm) across, and the minute spaces a foot (30 cm) square.

The minute hands, made of copper, are 14 feet (4.3 metres) long and weigh 224 pounds (102 kilograms) each. They travel the equivalent of 118 miles (190 kilometres) every year.

The hour hands, made of gunmetal, are 9 feet (2.7 metres) long and weigh nearly 700 pounds (317 kilograms) each.

There are three clock **weights**, weighing 2½ tons in total.

The clock **mechanism** weighs 5 tons.

The pendulum is 13 feet (3.9 metres) long, weighs 661 pounds (300 kilograms) and beats every two seconds.

Is it accurate? When the idea of a clock was first mooted, the Astronomer Royal insisted that it should be accurate to within one second – an extraordinary challenge at that time, and the Great Clock achieved it. To this day it is rarely as much as a second out. It's adjusted by putting old pennies in the tray at the top of the pendulum. Adding one old penny will make the Clock gain two-fifths of a second in 24 hours.

It is wound three times a week by hand, on Mondays, Wednesdays and Fridays. The winding takes more than an hour.

In August and September 2007 both the strike train (which rings the bells) and the going train (which controls the time-keeping) were overhauled. The Clock hands were driven by an electric motor, and the hour and quarter bells were silent. Abseilers repaired and cleaned the clock faces, and a photograph of four of them spreadeagled on the west face formed one of the House of Commons cards for Christmas 2007.

The Clock Tower was chosen in a poll in 2008 as Britain's favourite landmark. Stonehenge came second.

⊰ THE CHIMES OF THE GREAT CLOCK ⊱

The clock's chimes are to the lines:
> *Lord, through this hour,*
> *Be Thou our Guide,*
> *That through Thy power,*
> *No foot shall slide.*

The tune is the same as a phrase in the accompaniment to Handel's aria 'I know that my Redeemer liveth', from his oratorio *Messiah*. But it is more likely that the tune was composed by two undergraduates of Trinity College, Cambridge in about 1793 for the new clock in the University Church of Great St Mary. One of the two was William Crotch, a prolific composer of church music. The chime was used for the Royal Exchange in London, and then for the Great Clock at Westminster (and for countless clocks around the world). Whether by Handel or by Crotch and his friend, the tune has probably had more performances than any other.

Big Ben (the Great Bell) sounds the note E. The notes sounded by the Quarter Bells are:
1. G sharp
2. F sharp
3. E
4. B

From the start of the chime to the 12th strike takes 95 seconds. From the start of the hour strike to the 12th strike takes 54 seconds.

Big Ben was tolled for the first time for the funeral of King Edward VII in 1910. The Clock Tower bells were silent from 9.45am to midnight on 30 January 1965, the day of Sir Winston Churchill's funeral.

EXCHANGE CLOCKMAKER T   HE QUEEN, FROM THE DESIGNS OF EDMUND BECKETT DENISON   C.

The strike train (chiming mechanism) of the Great Clock

⊰ THE ANNUNCIATORS ⊱

The annunciators showing the item of business before the House of Commons, and the Member speaking, were introduced in 1894, ingenious arrangements of inked hammers which spelled out the information on a rolling paper tape. By 1939 there were 19 sets; and when the system gave way to CCTV in 1968 there were 46 receivers. One remains as an exhibit by the exit to the Terrace.

There are now 3,000 TV screens serving the Commons. A similar system operates in the Lords, and both systems make naval noises to announce a new piece of information: the Commons *bong* is a G, the note sounded by a Royal Marine bugler in a warship to herald an announcement; and the Lords *bong-bong . . . bong* is not unlike the striking of a ship's bell an hour-and-a-half into the four hours of a watch.

⊰ THE STATUE OF MARGARET THATCHER ⊱

The statue by Antony Dufort in the Members' Lobby was unveiled on 21 February 2007. It weighs 71 stone (451 kilograms), cost £80,000, and is made of silicon bronze. *I might have preferred iron*, said Thatcher at the unveiling. *But bronze will do. It won't rust.*

⚜ THE AYRTON LIGHT ⚜

At the top of the Clock Tower is the Ayrton Light, named after the first Commissioner of Works when it was installed. It is lit when the House of Commons is sitting after dark (that happens rather less these days with the changes to sitting hours and the programming of legislation). In Victorian times the light could be seen only from the West End of London, as that covered the smarter parts of London in which Members were presumed to live.

With London in blackout, the Ayrton Light was extinguished for almost the whole of the Second World War. It was relit on 24 April 1945 by Speaker Clifton Brown, who pressed a switch during a sitting of the House. Unusually, his speech appears in full in the *Journal* as well as in Hansard:

A Motion was made, and the Question being proposed, That this House do now adjourn. – (Mr Mathers.)

Mr Speaker addressed the House, as followeth:

May I be allowed to make a slight interruption in the proceedings?

In peace-time the lantern light above Big Ben always shone out after sunset to show that the House of Commons was at work. For five years, seven months and twenty-three days this light has now been extinguished.

When I press this switch our lantern light will shine once more. In doing so, I pray that, with God's blessing, this light will shine henceforth not only as an outward and visible sign that the Parliament of a free people is assembled in free debate, but also, that it may shine as a beacon of sure hope in a sadly torn and distracted world.

I now turn on our lantern light.

Ordered, *That what has now been said by Mr Speaker be entered upon the Journals of this House.* – (Mr Mathers.)

And the Question being put;

Resolved, *That this House do now adjourn.*

And accordingly the House, having continued to sit till sixteen minutes before Ten of the clock, adjourned till to-morrow.

The light on the Clock Tower, from the Illustrated London News, *1875*

⊰ THE MACE ⊱

On 20 April 1653 Cromwell ejected the remaining Members of the Long (by then the Rump) Parliament, describing the **mace** as: *that shining bauble there.*

The Clerk of the House entered in the *Journal*: *This day His Excellency the Lord General dissolved this Parliament*. But six years later the House ordered that this entry should be expunged from the *Journal*, on the grounds that only the Crown could dissolve Parliament. The manuscript of the *Journal*, still preserved in the Parliamentary Archives, shows that the expunging was done very enthusiastically; it is almost impossible to read what had been written.

The 'Bauble' Mace was relatively new; it had been specially made in 1649 when after the execution of the King the Commons wanted a mace with the arms of the Commonwealth. Following the restoration of Charles II, a new mace was made with his arms. Although the mace was changed again at least six times, on the last occasion in 1819, the 1660 mace was brought back, and this is the one which is used to this day.

◄ THE GIFTS OF THE COMMONWEALTH ►

A new Commons Chamber (with offices above and below) was built between 1945 and 1950 to replace the Chamber destroyed in 1941. The Commons first sat in their new Chamber, designed by Sir Giles Gilbert Scott, on 26 October 1950. Present in the Gallery were Speakers from 28 Commonwealth countries, whose gifts had helped furnish the new building:

Aden: Members' Writing Room table.

Australia: Speaker's Chair, in black bean wood.

Bahamas: Minister's writing desk and chair.

Barbados: Minister's writing desk and chair.

Bermuda: two triple silver gilt inkstands.

Botswana: a silver gilt ashtray.

British Honduras: Minister's writing desk and chair and royal coat of arms.

Canada: Table of the House, in Canadian oak.

Ceylon: Serjeant at Arms's chair.

Cyprus: Members' Writing Room table.

Dominica: a silver gilt inkstand.

The Falkland Islands: a silver gilt ashtray.

Fiji: a silver gilt inkstand

The Gambia: two silver gilt ashtrays.

Ghana: Minister's writing desk and chair.

Gibraltar: two oak table lamps with bronze shades.

Grenada: a silver gilt inkstand.

Guernsey: Minister's writing desk and three chairs.

Guyana: four triple silver gilt inkstands.

Hong Kong: a triple silver gilt inkstand.

India: the entrance doors at one end of the Chamber.

Isle of Man: a silver gilt inkstand and two silver gilt ashtrays for the Prime Minister's Conference Room.

Jamaica: the Bar of the House, in bronze.

Jersey: Minister's writing desk and chair and silver gilt inkstand.

Kenya: Minister's writing desk and chair.

Leeward Islands: six oak table lamps with bronze shades.

Lesotho: two silver gilt ashtrays.

Malawi: a silver gilt inkstand and a silver gilt ashtray.

Malaya: Minister's writing desk and chair.

Malta: three silver gilt ashtrays.

Mauritius: Minister's writing desk and chair.

Newfoundland: six chairs for the Prime Minister's Conference Room.

New Zealand: two Despatch Boxes in pururi wood.

Nigeria: furniture for the Aye Division Lobby in iroko wood.

Northern Ireland: two clocks and a division clock for the Chamber.

Pakistan: the entrance doors at the other end of the Chamber.

Rhodesia: two silver gilt inkstands with paper racks.

Sabah: a table and five chairs for interview room.

⊰ THE FIRST TRAFFIC LIGHTS IN THE UK ⊱

The first traffic lights were installed in Parliament Square in December 1868. Devised by the railway engineer J.P. Knight, they consisted of rotating green and red lanterns with semaphore arms. They were a less than encouraging precedent because they exploded less than a year later, injuring the policeman who was operating them.

In 1926, Parliament Square became the **first 'official' roundabout** in the UK.

⊰ GREEN AND RED ⊱

Every visitor to the Palace of Westminster notices that **the Houses are colour-coded**. Red for the Lords, green for the Commons: whether carpets, writing-paper or – most evidently – the benches in the two Chambers. Red for the Lords is easy enough as red is a royal colour and it would be natural for it to be used for an assembly where the king met his chief nobles.

No-one knows for certain why the Commons colour should be green. Did it derive from the livery colours of the Tudors (green and white)? Certainly in the 13th century, St Stephen's Chapel (where the Commons sat 300 years later) was painted green, but in the 14th century it was a blaze of colours, with a blue ceiling on which were gilded stars.

For whatever reason, green was an established Commons colour by the 17th century. A French traveller described the House in 1663 as: *une chamber mediocrement grande, environrée de six or sept rangs de dégrez, couverts de sarge vert* ('a moderately large room, surrounded by six or seven tiered rows of seats, covered in green serge'); and the Lord Chamberlain's accounts for 1672–1673 record the purchase of green cloth for the Commons Chamber.

A century later a German traveller saw *all round the sides of the House under the gallery are benches for the Members, covered in green cloth, always one above the other, like choirs in our churches.* By the 19th century the benches were covered in leather, as they are today.

When you walk through the Palace, as one colour gives

way to another, you know that you have entered the territory of the other House. There is one exception: the Pugin Room, where tea is served in the afternoon and drinks at lunchtime and in the evening, has a red carpet but is territory firmly claimed by the Commons following a deal about Committee Rooms a century or so ago. This is still not accepted by the Lords, but change seems unlikely.

III

COMMONS AND LORDS

I am dead, dead. But in the Elysian Fields.
Benjamin Disraeli, describing the House of Lords
shortly after becoming Earl of Beaconsfield

*The great speakers fill me with despair, and
the bad ones with terror.*
Edward Gibbon, the historian, about the House of
Commons (of which he was a Member for
eight years but never made a speech)

⚔ THE FIRST SPEAKER ⚔

The first speaker who was known as the Speaker of the
House of Commons was Sir Thomas Hungerford in 1376,
the *Chivaler qi avoit les paroles pur les Comunes
d'Engleterre en cest Parlement* ('the knight who was the
spokesman for the Commons of England in this
Parliament'), although others acted as conveners, and
perhaps spokesmen, before then (probably beginning with
Peter de Montfort at the Mad Parliament in 1258).

⊰ THE FIRST CLERK OF ⊱
THE HOUSE OF COMMONS

The first Clerk was Robert de Melton, appointed 'Under-Clerk of the Parliaments, to wait upon the Commons', in 1363. His salary was £5 a year for life.

⊰ HOW MANY MEMBERS? ⊱

The House of Commons had around **250 Members** as early as the 15th century – two knights from each of 37 counties, two citizens or burgesses from each of more than 80 cities and boroughs, and 14 from the Cinque Ports.

By 1673 the House – representing only England and Wales – had **513 MPs**. 300 of their constituencies were either controlled or owned outright by Members of the House of Lords.

Adding Scotland by the Act of Union of 1707 increased the number to **558**.

Adding Ireland with the Union of 1801 increased the number to **658**.

In 1885 the size of the House increased again to **670**, and reached its highest total of **707** in 1918.

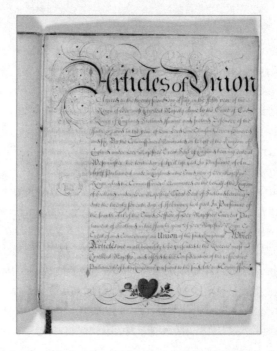

The English copy of the Articles of Union between England and Scotland, 1707

By 1922 Irish independence had reduced the numbers to **615**, but the 20th century saw a gradual increase to **659** by 1997, falling to **646** (taking account of Scottish devolution) in 2005.

There are now **529** MPs in England, 59 in Scotland, 40 in Wales and 18 in Northern Ireland.

⚜ REFORM ⚜

The First Reform Bill was read a second time on 21 March 1831 after two days' debate and by a majority of one. Macaulay described the scene:

> *The Tellers scarcely got through the crowd, for the House was thronged to the Table . . . But you might have heard a pin drop as Duncannon read the numbers. Then again the shouts broke out and many of us shed tears. I could scarcely refrain. And the jaw of Peel fell and the face of Twiss was as the face of a damned soul; and Herries looked like Judas, taking his necktie off for the last operation. We shook hands and clapped each other on the back and went out, crying and huzzaing into the Lobby. And no sooner were the doors opened than another shout answered that within the House.*

'The Champions of Reform [Grey and Brougham] destroying the Monster of Corruption [Wellington and Peel]', 1831

⚜ **VIEWS OF THE HOUSE OF LORDS** ⚜

Disraeli said of the House of Lords (despite the quotation at the head of this chapter):

> *It reminds me of nothing so much as a ducal household . . . with His Grace lying dead in an upper Chamber.*

Walter Bagehot, the 19th-century journalist and writer on the constitution:

> *The use of the House of Lords, or rather, of the Lords, in its dignified capacity – is very great. It does not attract such reverence as the Queen, but it attracts very much. The office of an order of nobility is to impose on the common people – not necessarily to impose on them what is untrue, yet less what is hurtful; but still to impose on their quiescent imaginations what would not otherwise be there. The fancy of the mass of men is incredibly weak; it can see nothing without a visible symbol and there is much it can scarcely make out with a symbol. Nobility is the symbol of mind. It has the marks from which the mass of men always used to infer mind, and often still infer it.*
>
> *A common clever man who goes into a country place will get no reverence; but the 'old squire' will get reverence. Even after he is insolvent, when every one knows that his ruin is but a question of time, he will get five times as much respect from the common peasantry as the newly-made rich man who sits beside him. The common peasantry will listen to his nonsense more submissively than the new man's sense. An old lord will get infinite respect.*

Bagehot also quoted *a severe though not unfriendly critic of our institutions* who said that *the cure for admiring the House of Lords was to go and look at it.*

Stephen Leacock's view:

> *The Parliament buildings are so vast that it is not possible to state with certainty what they do, or do not, contain. But it is generally said that somewhere in the building is the House of Lords. When they meet they are said to come together very quietly shortly before the dinner hour, take a glass of dry sherry and a biscuit (they are all abstemious men), reject whatever bills may be before them at the moment, take another dry sherry, and then adjourn for another two years.*

My Discovery of England, 1922

The House of Lords is like a glass of champagne that has stood for five days.

Attributed to **Clement Attlee**

During the 1968 debates on the future of the House of Lords, **Enoch Powell** said:

> *It is not for anything; it just is, like an oak tree. You don't ask what an oak tree is for, do you?*

⊰ WHAT ARE THE BOOKS ON THE TABLE ⊱
OF THE HOUSE OF COMMONS?

The morocco-bound volumes between the two Despatch Boxes are largely decorative. They are Acts of Parliament between 1981 and 1996. Also on the Table, in green slip-covers, are copies of *Erskine May*, *Dod's Parliamentary Companion*, *Vacher's Guide*, *the Standing Orders* and the *Register of Members' Interests*. The Despatch Boxes themselves are made of the New Zealand wood pururi (*Vitex lucens*).

⊰ IS THERE ANYTHING IN ⊱
THE DESPATCH BOXES?

On the Government side, the Despatch Box has copies (in English – and English in Braille, Welsh, Gaelic and Cornish) of the Oath of Allegiance sworn by MPs when they first come into the House, and then after each general election, and the Affirmation (for those MPs who do not wish to swear).

The Oath is:
> *I do swear that I will be faithful and bear true allegiance to Her Majesty Queen Elizabeth, her heirs and successors, according to law. So help me God.*

Also in the Despatch Box is a New Testament, a Douai Bible (for Roman Catholics) and an Old Testament (for Jews). Kept safely away from the Chamber, in cases so that they cannot be handled by infidels, is a Koran for Muslims and a Granth Sahib for Sikhs.

There is nothing in the Despatch Box on the Opposition side.

The Chamber of the House of Commons, from the Opposition Despatch Box

⊰ CANDLES ⊱

In former times the business of the House of Commons could be interrupted by a motion *That **candles** be brought in*; but by an order of 1717 the Serjeant at Arms was given the duty of having the House lighted when *daylight be shut in.* In the 21st century this duty would be discharged by providing emergency lanterns in the event of a power failure.

⊰ HOW MANY PEERS? ⊱

On 1 July 2009 the House of Lords contained:
- 2 Archbishops
- 24 Bishops
- 23 Law Lords
- 600 Life Peers
- 91 Peers 'under the House of Lords Act 1999' (the former hereditaries)
- 12 Peers had leave of absence
- 2 Peers were suspended
- 1 peer was disqualified by being an MEP

Total 755

The state of the parties was:

Labour	214
Conservative	196
Cross-Bench (independent)	201
Liberal Democrat	71

⊰ THE *JOURNAL* OF THE HOUSE OF ⊱ COMMONS

The *Journal* is compiled from the manuscript *Minute Book* kept by the Clerks at the Table. It is the legal record of what the House has decided rather than what is said (which goes into Hansard). It is usually pretty laconic. The fall of the Callaghan Government and the start of the Thatcher era is described thus in the *Journal* (28 March 1979):

> *No confidence in Her Majesty's Government, – A Motion was made, and the Question being put, That this House has no confidence in Her Majesty's Government – (Mrs Margaret Thatcher);*
> *The House divided.*
> *Tellers for the Ayes, Mr Spencer Le Marchant, Mr Michael Roberts: 311.*
> *Tellers for the Noes, Mr James Hamilton, Mr Donald Coleman: 310.*
> *So the Question was agreed to.*
> *Resolved, That this House has no confidence in Her Majesty's Government.*

In 1621 the House sentenced someone who had offended it to be hanged, drawn and quartered. The unfortunate individual and his friends petitioned the House for mercy. They were only fairly successful. The *Journal* recorded:
House inclined to mercy. Ordered, That his head be severed from his body only.

MPs might today regret the passing of the parliamentary power to punish journalists and demonstrators. In the 17th century it was routine – from the *Journal* (4 November 1652):

Mr Speaker, by way of report, informed the Parliament, That, as he was coming to do his duty in Parliament one Solomon Arnold threw a brick, which hit the Serjeant's Mace and narrowly escaped hitting the Serjeant on the head, as he waited on Mr Speaker, and threw another stone, which hit Mr Speaker on the face.

Resolved, That the said Solomon Arnold be brought to the Bar as a delinquent.

Ordered, That the said Solomon Arnold be committed to Bridewell, London, there to be kept to hard labour, and daily corrected, until the Parliament take further order.

The sufferings of the Serjeant at Arms, from the *Journal* (26 January 1580):

The House being moved, that the Serjeant, having some defection of his Limbs, and being somewhat pained in his Feet, is licensed, by this House, to ride upon a Foot-cloth Nag.

From the index to the *Journal*:

Queen: *See under King.*
Clerk: *See under Table.*

There was not much of a Christmas recess in the Puritan years of the 17th century. From the *Journal* (11 December 1648):

> *Resolved, That the House will adjourn for Christmas Eve and Christmas Day only.*

And from the *Journal* (24 December 1652):

> *Resolved, That no observation shall be had on 25th day of December, commonly called Christmas Day, nor any solemnity used or exercised in Churches, upon that day, in respect thereof.*
>
> *Ordered, That the Committee of Whitehall do see that the shops in Westminster Hall be kept open to-morrow.*

The Clerks at the Table recorded what the House decided; but also from time to time artistic detail. From the *Journal* (31 May 1604):

> *During the argument of this Bill, a young Jackdaw flew into the House – called Malum Omen to this Bill.*

From the *Journal* (5 November 1605):

> *This last night the Upper House of Parliament was searched by Sir Thos. Knyvett; and one Johnson, a servant to Mr Thomas Percy, was there apprehended, who had placed thirty-six barrels of gunpowder in the vault under the House, with a purpose to blow up the King, and the whole Company, when they should there assemble. Afterwards divers other gentlemen were discovered to be of the plot.*

And from the *Journal* (14 May 1606):

> *A Dog comes in: A strange Spanyell, of Mouse-colour, came into the House.*

❧ A DIFFERENT APPROACH TO ❧
RECORDING EVENTS

Shortly after Lloyd George succeeded Asquith as Prime Minister, he presided at a long and difficult meeting of the War Cabinet. They then adjourned for dinner. LG said to the Secretary of the Cabinet, Sir Maurice Hankey, *You know what we've agreed, Maurice. Do a note, would you?* When Cabinet returned, Hankey's note read:

> *Now while the great ones depart for their dinner,*
> *The Secretary stays on, growing thinner and thinner.*
> *Racking his brains to record and report*
> *What he thinks that they think that they ought to have thought.*

❧ THE LONGEST SPEAKERSHIP ❧

The longest speakership was that of Arthur Onslow, first chosen Speaker in 1727, re-elected four times and finally retiring in 1761. Onslow is credited with establishing the political impartiality of the Speakership.

❧ 'THE OTHER PLACE' ❧

'The other place' is often thought to be the required term for the House of Lords when mentioned in debate in the House of Commons, but there is no such requirement. It is perfectly in order to say 'the House of Lords'.

Civil servant's note on a ministerial brief, read out by mistake. Quoted by Lord Home in *The Way the Wind Blows* (1976):

> *This is a rotten argument, but it should be good enough for their Lordships on a hot summer afternoon.*

David Lloyd George in the House of Commons, 21 December 1908:

> *The House of Lords is not the watchdog of the Constitution; it is Mr Balfour's poodle. It fetches and carries for him. It barks for him. It bites anyone that he sets it on to.*

Harold Macmillan, 1st Earl of Stockton:

> *If, like me, you are over ninety, frail, on two sticks, half deaf and half blind, you stick out like a sore thumb in most places, but not in the House of Lords.*

⊰ SOME HOUSE OF COMMONS STATISTICS ⊱

In the financial year 2008–09:

The House sat for **149 days**; the average sitting was **seven hours and 37 minutes**.

The average length of the working papers for each day's sitting (including Early Day Motions, Questions tabled the previous day and amendment papers for Public Bill Committees as well as the core working papers for the House itself) was **353 pages**.

An average of **85 Early Day Motions** were tabled each week, and an average of **3,884 signatures** added to Motions each week.

There were **25 Government Bills** and **98 Private Members' Bills**. **6,508 amendments** were tabled.

There were **1,123 meetings** of select committees.

The Parliament website www.parliament.uk received **51 million requests** (more than double the figure for 2003–04).

⊰ MEMBERS OF PARLIAMENT ⊱
WERE FIRST PAID

MPs first received payment to attend Parliament in the 13th century, when shires and boroughs paid four shillings a day [2009 equivalent, £106] to knights and two shillings a day to citizens and burgesses. Some got more: in 1296 the two Aldermen representing the City of London received the sum of 10 shillings [£266] a day.

The payment was not always in money: in 1463 the Borough of Weymouth paid its burgesses 500 mackerel. Not all at the same time, one imagines . . .

The poet Andrew Marvell was supposedly the last person to receive a salary under these rather informal arrangements: he was paid by the Borough of Kingston upon Hull until his death in 1678.

Payment for Members was seen as a way of ensuring that your MP went to Parliament and told you what was going on. Samuel Pepys records in his *Diary* (30 March 1668):

> *At dinner . . . all concluded that the bane of the Parliament hath been the leaving off the old custom of the places allowing wages to those that served them in Parliament, by which they chose men that understood their business and would attend it, and they could expect an account from, which now they cannot.*

In modern times MPs were first paid in 1911, at the rate of £400 a year (2009 equivalent, £22,824). This salary was reduced to £360 in 1931 and returned to £400 only in 1935. The rate payable from 1 April 2009 is £64,766.

⚔ IN THE HOUSE TOO LONG ⚔

Maurice Edelman, novelist and Labour MP, said that a Member of Parliament knew that he had been in the House too long when he realised that the words with which the Speaker usually moves on to the main business (*The Clerk will now proceed to read the Orders of the Day*) and the words with which some Member makes an immediate attempt to raise an issue (*Point of Order, Mr Speaker*) fitted perfectly to the tune of 'John Brown's Body'.

⚔ CHARACTERS ⚔

In my time I have never known the House of Commons without a funny man. Then there is the House of Commons bore – of course there is more than one, but there is always one par excellence; he is generally a man of encyclopaedic information which he has been unable to digest himself and which, therefore, he is always ready to impart to everybody else. Then you have the weighty man, and the gravity of the weighty man of the House of Commons is a thing to which there is no parallel in the world. You have the foolish man, the man with one idea, you have the independent man, you have the man who is a little cracked.

Joseph Chamberlain

There are lots of people I've encouraged and helped to get into the House of Commons. Looking at them now, I am not at all sure that it was a wise thing to do.

James Callaghan

⊰ *POUR ENCOURAGER* ⊱

When a court martial sentenced Admiral Byng to death for cowardice, William Pitt the Elder, then Leader of the House of Commons, told King George II that *The House of Commons, Sir, is inclined to mercy.* The King replied: *You have taught me to look for the sense of my people elsewhere than in the House of Commons.* Byng was shot on the quarterdeck of HMS *Monarch* on 14 March 1757.

⊰ A SENSE OF PRIORITIES ⊱

From *Country Life* (10 October 1908):
Next week Parliament will reassemble. The politicians who are at the head of the Government may think it necessary that this should be done; but the country gentleman as a rule looks upon an autumn session as an unmitigated nuisance. It takes him up to Town at a time when both sport and duty call for his presence at home; for when he is the

owner of a great estate, it is in the pleasant days between now and Christmas that he has the chance of walking over his land and finding how his tenants have been treating it and what improvements may be necessary. Furthermore, the duties of the autumn session are only such as a man performs for the sake of his conscience.

⊰ THE LONGEST-LIVED FORMER MPs ⊱

The longest-lived former MPs were Theodore Cooke Taylor, a Yorkshire mill owner and former Liberal MP who died in 1952 aged 102; and Bert Hazell, former Labour MP for North Norfolk, who died in 2009 aged 101.

⊰ THE LONDON MARATHON ⊱

The marathon has been run by 41 MPs: 20 Labour; 18 Conservative; two Lib Dem; and Paul Marsden (who ran two as a Labour MP and three as a Lib Dem); 40 men plus Patsy Calton, the Lib Dem MP who died in 2005.

Matthew Parris, then Conservative MP for West Derbyshire, ran in the first London Marathon in 1981, and in the next four races, improving his time in each one and ending with the best time for an MP of 2 hours 32 minutes 57 seconds.

In 2009 three MPs ran: Chris Bryant (Labour; 3 hours 50 minutes); Edward Timpson (Conservative; 3 hours 58 minutes); and Howard Stoate (Labour; 4 hours 10 minutes).

⊰ GURNEY'S SHORTHAND ⊱

What did Charles Dickens, Isambard Kingdom Brunel and Ebenezer Howard, the founder of the Garden City movement, have in common? Answer: they could all write **Gurney's shorthand**.

In the 1730s Thomas Gurney invented a system of shorthand which for the first time meant that a reliable verbatim record of meetings could be taken – before then memory and précis played a large part. This system of shorthand was immediately in demand both in the courts and in Parliament. In 1813 William Brodie Gurney, Thomas's grandson, became the official Shorthand Writer to the Houses of Parliament, so beginning the longest contract in English legal history, that between W.B. Gurney and Sons and Parliament.

Gurney's system of shorthand is no longer in use; Pitman's shorthand a century later allowed more accurate recording at faster speeds. The last Gurney's shorthand-writer left

Gurney's in the 1960s, and the last person to be able to read Gurney's shorthand left in the 1980s.

There is one 'short form' from Gurney's shorthand still in use: a circle representing the world, either around or over the outline for 'all' to mean 'all over the world' or 'all round the world'.

Charles Dickens said of his time as a Parliamentary reporter:

> *I have worn my knees by writing on them in the back row of the old Press Gallery. I have worn my feet standing to write in the preposterous pen in the old House of Lords where we used to huddle together like so many sheep, kept in waiting until the Woolsack might want restuffing.*

⊰ RELIEF FROM THE CARES OF OFFICE ⊱

On 30 January 1933, Adolf Hitler became Chancellor of Germany. A few days before, **Neville Chamberlain** wrote a letter to the Editor of *The Times*:

From the Chancellor of the Exchequer

> *Sir,*
> *It may be of interest to record that, in walking through St James's Park today, I noticed a grey wagtail running*

about on the now temporarily dry bed of the lake, near the dam below the bridge, and occasionally picking small insects out of the cracks in the dam.

Probably the occurrence of this bird in the heart of London has been recorded before, but I have not myself noted it in the Park.

I am your obedient servant,
NEVILLE CHAMBERLAIN
January 24th, 1933

P.S. For the purpose of removing doubts, as we say in the House of Commons, I should perhaps add that I mean a grey wagtail and not a pied.

IV

DEBATE AND DISPUTE

The practice of the House of Commons is . . . as wisely constructed for governing the debates of a deliberative body and obtaining its true sense as any which can become known to us.
Thomas Jefferson, third President of the United States

⊰ POINTS OF ORDER ⊱

Sir Walter Bromley-Davenport (1903–1989, MP for Knutsford): *I am not raising a point of order, Mr Speaker. I am raising a point of order on points of order that are not points of order.*
Mr Speaker: *Order. Points of order on points of order that are not points of order are not points of order.*

⊰ WHAT DOESN'T GET INTO HANSARD ⊱

The Official Report (also known as Hansard after T.C. Hansard, the 19th-century printer and publisher who produced a private-enterprise record of debates) does not record everything said in the House of Commons. It follows the rule set down by a select committee in 1907, and though *not strictly verbatim, is substantially the verbatim report, with repetitions and redundancies omitted, but which on the other hand leaves out nothing that adds to the meaning of the speech or illustrates the argument.*

In practice, Hansard records interjections only when the MP speaking responds to them. It misses some treasures:

James Hill (a rather large Conservative backbencher, moving the second reading of a Private Bill about which he had been heavily criticised): *And, I may say, I have been* personally *targeted.*

Tony Banks (Labour): *Blimey, that was 'ardly precision bombing.*

Nicholas Soames (as an Agriculture Minister, answering a Question on the preservation of rural England): *It is not our intention to cover the countryside in aspic.*

Tony Banks (Labour): *If it was, you'd* eat *it.*

Nicholas Soames himself has been a good contributor to the genre. When Paul Boateng, Labour Chief Secretary to the Treasury, appeared at the Despatch Box in a new, snappy, shiny suit, Soames boomed: *Boateng! Final fitting Friday.*

But Banksy (Tony Banks, Labour MP 1983–2005, created Lord Stratford 2005, died 2006) remains a legend:

- As Sports Minister, facing the bouffant-haired Peter Ainsworth across the Despatch Box: *I haven't come here to be insulted by a man with a Kevin Keegan haircut.*
- Of John Major when Prime Minister: *If he was an undertaker, people would stop dying.*
- Of Sir John Stokes, Conservative MP for Halesowen and Stourbridge: *One of the last genuine political cave-dwellers in this country.*
- About himself: *Good taste was never one of my qualifications.*
- When choosing his title: *I'd have preferred Lord Banks of the Thames.*
- As a vegetarian: *I never want to eat anything that has a face or a family.*

Banks, a stylish dresser, once remarked of an intervention in a debate: *I regard the honourable Gentleman's observation as an insult.* A Hansard reporter sent a message down to ask who had called him *a Marxist-Leninist stooge.* Banks replied: *He didn't call me a Marxist-Leninist stooge. He said I was wearing a Marks and Spencer suit.*

Colonel Sir Harwood Harrison (1907–1980, MP for Eye in Suffolk 1951–1979) was run over by a bus in Whitehall while chairman of the All-Party Parliamentary Road Safety Group. The bus was off the road for longer than Sir Harwood was in hospital.

⊰ **UNPARLIAMENTARY LANGUAGE** ⊱

Erskine May says: *Good temper and moderation are the characteristics of Parliamentary language.* Many people (and many MPs) think that there is a list of **words that one cannot use in debate**. Not true. There was a list in *Erskine May* up to its 19th edition in 1983, but it was dropped because the context of a word can be as important as the word itself. The main no-nos today are (a) 'hypocrisy' and imputing false motives (b) misrepresenting what someone has said (c) charges of *deliberately* lying (misleading, if not deliberate, is not itself unparliamentary) and (d) abusive or insulting language.

Sir Thomas Erskine May, 1st Lord Farnborough, Clerk of the House of Commons 1871–1886

Churchill got round the prohibition on 'lie' by renaming it *a terminological inexactitude.*

Richard Brinsley Sheridan is supposed to have responded to a rebuke from the Chair by saying:

Mr Speaker, I said the honourable Member was a liar it is true and I am sorry for it. The honourable Member may place the punctuation where he pleases.

There may no longer be a list of unparliamentary expressions in *Erskine May,* but every year in *The Table*, the journal of the Society of Clerks-at-the-Table in Commonwealth Parliaments, the aficionado can find a priceless list of remarks given a red card by Speakers in Commonwealth Parliaments. Somehow the most memorable always seem to be in Australia:

- *Let me pick up the interjection by the moron from Geelong. (Victoria)*
- *You hypocritical bastard. (Australian Capital Territory)*
- *You great, flap-eared dork. You really are a dill. (New South Wales)*
- *The right honourable gentleman's inconsistency sticks out like a shag on a rock. (New South Wales)*
- *You are as crooked as the rest of them! (Victoria)*
- *Can you shut that prick up? (Victoria)*
- *If good news was a cow, this minister would be a cattle tick. (Northern Territory)*
- *I grew up just south of your electorate, Sport, so don't lecture me on what I do or do not know. (Victoria)*

Canada is sometimes close behind:

- *The minister should get his head out of the sand and stick it up his attic.* (Canadian House of Commons)
- *The Member for Gander got gum in his hair. Guess how it got there? The Premier had swallowed it.* (Newfoundland and Labrador House of Assembly)
- *For him to breathe these days, he has to have vents in his heels.* (Newfoundland and Labrador House of Assembly)
- *Pig plutocrat.* (Saskatchewan)

Sometimes one wonders quite what set the Chair off. For example, the following were ruled out of order:

- *Bob the Builder.* (New Zealand)
- *Unreliable fellows.* (Gujarat)
- *Comedy routine.* (Yukon)
- *If you cannot hear it, you have cloth ears.* (Northern Territory)
- *Party of old men.* (New Zealand)
- *Joker. (Rajya Sabha* (Indian Upper House))
- *I withdraw the word 'ignorant' and I will substitute it with 'uneducated'.* (British Columbia)
- *Tories.* (New Zealand)

⚔ **POLITICAL PATOIS: A GUIDE TO SOME** ⚔ **FREQUENTLY USED PHRASES**

I think that what is important is . . . = Sorry, I don't like that question. Could we talk about something else?

But we've moved on from there = I am trying very hard to forget all about this.

Let me clarify that = Let me say something completely different.

We've always made it perfectly clear that . . . = There was a ghastly row last week and we now have a completely new policy.

Hard-working families = Families.

Issue = Problem, cock-up, disaster.

Shortly = Not for a long time.

In due course = Never.

The honourable Member is a very experienced parliamentarian = The honourable Member has been here for far too long.

The honourable Member's enthusiasm for this subject is well known = The honourable Member is a crashing bore.

Roll-out = Gradual and uneven implementation which can be stopped if anything goes wrong. (The proper meaning – rolling a new aircraft out of the hangar – seems to have been long forgotten; but it is worth remembering that in a 'roll-out' the aircraft doesn't actually have to fly.)

Going forward, as in *this will be a requirement going forward* = A phrase intended to convey an impression of dynamic action, but in fact devoid of meaning.

⊷ CATCHING THE SPEAKER'S EYE ⊷

All MPs seek to do this, whether to ask a question or to speak in a debate. In the distant past the Speaker would not call a Member by name, but simply look meaningfully at the person he intended to call.

This practice is supposed to have ended with Sir John Trevor, Speaker from 1685 to 1687 and from 1690 to 1695, who was expelled from the House for taking bribes. Trevor had so bizarre a squint that when he looked meaningfully at the Member he intended to call, MPs in various parts of the Chamber would assume that the choice had fallen upon them.

Nowadays the occupant of the Chair says simply *Mr Such-and-such* and there is no doubt. Not usually, at any rate:

Mr Speaker: *Mr what's-his-name? – Bruinvels.*
Mr Bruinvels (Leicester East): *I can confirm that I am standing up, Mr Speaker.*
Mr Speaker: *My sincere apologies. We all make mistakes.*

Hansard (29 January 1987)

Speaker Shaw-Lefevre, Speaker from 1839 to 1857, was once asked how he picked the right man to carry on the debate when so many stood to catch his eye. *Well,* he replied, *I have not been shooting all my life for nothing, and I have learned to mark the right one.*

⊰ WHIPS ⊱

Whips or whippers-in were originally those who maintained order and discipline in the hunting field. Since the middle of the 19th century the term has been used of those who maintain discipline in a parliamentary party, as well as providing intelligence and advice to the party leadership. And discipline – especially in the House of Commons – includes being there when expected, and voting as expected. *The Whip* is the weekly list of business circulated by the Whips of a party to each of their MPs. The level of expectation is indicated by one, two or three lines under the request for an MP's presence. A three-line Whip is ignored at your peril.

To: Members and Members' Staff

SECRET - Whip

23rd April 2009

MONDAY 27th APRIL
Last day for tabling: **Innovation, Universities and Skills; Scotland**
House meets at **2.30pm** for Oral Questions: **Children, Schools and Families**
Ten Minute Rule Motion: Cheapest Energy Tariff (Information)
Continuation of the Budget Debate
THERE WILL BE A **1-LINE WHIP**

TUESDAY 28th APRIL
Last day for tabling: **Justice**
House meets at **2.30pm** for Oral Questions: **Treasury**
Ten Minute Rule Motion: Protection of Children (Publicity)
Conclusion of the Budget Debate
THERE WILL BE A **3-LINE WHIP at 9.30pm for 10.00pm**

WEDNESDAY 29th APRIL
Last day for tabling: **Prime Minister (at 1.00pm)**
House meets at **11.30am** for Oral Questions: **Wales**
At 12.00 noon: Prime Minister's Questions
Ten Minute Rule Motion: Prevention of Excessive Charges
Opposition Day (10th Allotted Day)
1.   The Erosion of Civil Liberties and Freedoms Followed by
2.   The situation in Sri Lanka Both Debates will arise on a Liberal Democrat Motion
THERE WILL BE A **2-LINE WHIP at 3.30pm for 4.00pm and 6.30pm for 7.00pm**

THURSDAY 30th APRIL
Last day for tabling: **Business, Enterprise and Regulatory Reform; Church Commissioners, Public Accounts Commission and Speaker's Committee on the Electoral Commission**
House meets at **10.30am** for Oral Questions: **Innovation, Universities and Skills**
House Business
THERE WILL BE A **2-LINE WHIP from 12.30pm**

FRIDAY 1st MAY
The House will not be sitting

An extract from a party Whip

W.S. Gilbert took a dig at party discipline in *Iolanthe*. When the curtain rises on Act II, Private Willis is discovered on sentry duty outside Westminster Hall:

When in that House MPs divide,
If they've a brain, and cerebellum too,
They've got to leave that brain outside,
And vote just as their leaders tell 'em to.
But then the prospect of a lot
Of dull MPs in close proximity,
All thinking for themselves, is what
No man can face with equanimity.

Iolanthe **was first performed** on 25 November 1882, in the presence of the Prince of Wales and – rather more surprisingly – Mr Gladstone, then two years into his second Prime Ministership.

Gladstone might have appreciated Gilbert's go at the House of Lords:

When Wellington thrashed Bonaparte,
As every child can tell,
The House of Peers, throughout the war,
Did nothing in particular,
And did it very well . . .

And while the House of Peers withholds
Its legislative hand,
And noble statesmen do not itch
To interfere with matters which
They do not understand,

As bright will shine Great Britain's rays
As in King George's golden days!

⊰ HATS ⊱

For much of parliamentary history, **headgear** played a greater part – both sartorial and symbolic – than it does today. Hats were normally worn in the Chamber, but not while speaking. The Duke of Wellington said of the Parliament following the passing of the first Reform Bill: *I never saw so many shocking bad hats in my life.*

In the 19th-century Commons, the **tall silk hat** which was an essential part of any gentleman's attire started to be used to reserve places in the Chamber (there being no allotted seats). As with any such practice, it was open to abuse, and the unscrupulous used a second hat for the purpose.

In 1900 a Member described the conventions thus (with apparently no satirical intent):
> *At all times remove your hat on entering the House, and put it on upon taking your seat; and remove it again on rising for whatever purpose. If the MP asks a question he will stand, and with his hat off; and he may receive the answer of the Minister seated and with his hat on. If on a division he should have to challenge the ruling of the Chair, he will sit and put his hat on. If he wishes to address the Speaker on a point of order not connected*

with a division, he will do so standing with his hat off. When he leaves the House to participate in a division he will take his hat off, but will vote with it on. If the Queen sends a Message to be read from the Chair, the Member will uncover. In short, how to take his seat, how to behave at Prayers, and what to do with his hat, form between them the ABC of the Parliamentary scholar.

That convention that a Member raising a point of order during a division should be seated with a hat on persisted until late in the 20th century. Indeed, a collapsible opera hat was kept at the Serjeant at Arms's chair at the far end of the Chamber, and the rapid progress of the hat down the benches until it reached the Member who wished to raise a point of order was followed by the rather odd sight of a Member wearing a top hat trying to bring some alleged procedural irregularity to the attention of the Speaker.

So in 1976 the procedure was referred to the Procedure Committee amid considerable confidence that the hat would be consigned to history. At this point the Law of Unintended Consequences took a hand. So far from recommending the abolition of the hat, the Committee after considerable deliberation decided that the mischief was not in the hat procedure, but the difficulty in laying hold of a hat at the crucial moment. So they recommended that a **second hat** be acquired, and kept at the other end of the Chamber. But – perhaps as well for a televised House of Commons – the hats are no more.

◄ GIVING WAY ►

A tradition of the British Parliament, is that of a Member **'giving way'** during a speech, to allow an intervention by another Member. Interventions are often used to put a contrary point or to 'correct' something which has just been said. The intervention may come from anywhere in the House; the Member who has the floor does not have to give way, but once he or she has done so, the Member intervening has the right to speak.

Giving way can make a debate much livelier than the mere reading out of contributions; and it is noticeable that Members who rely on a script find it much harder to deal with interventions.

◄ THE INVENTION OF THE CLOSURE ►

Nothing in the last 130 years has matched the stormy days of January and February 1881, when Gladstone's Government was attempting to proceed with the Protection of Person and Property (Ireland) Bill, and was encountering obstruction and disruption of proceedings from a group of Irish Nationalist Members. The debate on the Queen's Speech had occupied 11 days (mostly on Irish matters). The motion for bringing in the Bill was debated for five more days, and might have continued for much longer; but in the small hours of Wednesday 2 February (the motion having been debated for 41 hours), the Speaker, Sir Henry Brand, said to the House:

The usual rules have proved powerless to ensure orderly and effective Debate. An important measure, recommended in Her Majesty's Speech nearly a month since, and declared to be urgent, in the interests of the State, by a decisive majority, is being arrested by the action of an inconsiderable minority . . .

The dignity, the credit and the authority of this House are seriously threatened, and it is necessary that they should be vindicated. Under the operation of the accustomed rules and methods of procedure, the legislative powers of the House are paralysed. A new and exceptional course is imperatively demanded; and I am satisfied that I shall best carry out the will of the House, and may rely upon its support, if I decline to call upon any more Members to speak, and at once put the Questions from the Chair.

Pandemonium followed; an eyewitness described *tumultuous cheering*, and the Bill was introduced. This was the first use of **'the closure'** – the proposal that *The question be now put* which still remains a means of bringing any debate to an end and a decision being taken. In Victorian times it had to be approved by a majority of three to one; these days a simple majority suffices (although at least 100 Members have to vote in the majority – a requirement that has led to many a Private Member's Bill being 'talked out' on a Friday afternoon).

⚜ EARLY DAY MOTIONS (EDMs) ⚜

Early Day Motions are an opportunity for MPs to table an expression of view for debate on 'an early day' – in other words, for some unspecified future occasion. This usually means that the motion will probably never be debated. Very few ever are; they are mostly technical motions required to trigger the consideration of some statutory instrument in committee upstairs. But if the Opposition put down a motion of no confidence in the Government of the day, this may appear briefly as an EDM (as did the motion on which the Callaghan Government fell in 1979).

EDMs are subject to the usual rules of order, and may not be longer than 250 words. They are used for every purpose imaginable: to attack the Government, the policies of the Opposition, the behaviour or utterances of an individual MP; to draw attention to the work of a pressure group or charity; to mark an anniversary or 'World Something Day'; to pass an opinion on an event, whether triumph or disaster; to comment on the doings of others (such as the BBC and Jonathan Ross); to put forward a new idea or to call for solutions to some problem; even to congratulate an MP's local football team.

Between 2,000 and 3,000 EDMs are tabled every year; every sitting day the Table Office takes an average of 17 new ones, and some 860 names of MPs to be added to those already tabled.

In 2006 an EDM which consisted entirely of a specially written poem by Roger McGough was ruled out of order by the Chair, largely because it could not form a decision to which the House could come if it were ever debated (and in that event it might have been a novel task for the Chair to decide whether amendments were out of order if they did not scan . . .).

But in 1990 the following EDM was allowed; indeed, it could hardly have been refused given that it was directly concerned with a piece of legislation, although of a highly unusual kind . . . *and* it attracted an amendment:

No.74   Notices of Motions: 19th March 1990   2461

738 FOSSIL FUEL LEVY REGULATIONS

Mr Peter Hardy
Mr Martin Redmond
Mr George J. Buckley
Mr Jimmy Hood
Mr Frank Haynes
Mr Tom Cox

That this House views with concern the following extract from Schedule 2 of the Fossil Fuel Levy Regulations 1990: –

$$r_y = \frac{K_y + D_y''}{X_y''} \times 100$$

and
and
$$D_y'' = A_y'' - B_y'' + C_y'' - E_y'' - F_y'' + G_y''$$

$$K_y = \left[\left(D_{y-1}' - D_{y-1}''\right) - \frac{R_{y-1}}{100} \times \left(X_{y-1}' - X_{y-1}''\right) + \left(\frac{r_{y-1} - R_{y-1}}{100} \times X_{y-1}'' \right) \right] \times \left[1 + \frac{I_{y-1}}{100} \right]$$
$$+ \left[\left(D_{y-2} - D_{y-2}'\right) - \frac{R_{y-2}}{100} \times \left(X_{y-2} - X_{y-2}'\right) \right] \times \left[1 + \frac{I_{y-2}}{100} \right] \times \left[1 + \frac{I_{y-1}}{100} \right]$$

and
$$B_{yP} = \sum_n \sum_j (Y_{nj} \times Z_{nj}) + \sum_n \left[\left(V_n - \sum_j Y_{nj}\right) \times \left(\frac{\sum_j Z_{nj}}{W_n} \right) \right]$$

---

and wonders whether the average citizen or the school leaver who has followed the national curriculum or those honourable Members who voted for the privatisation of the electricity industry are able to comprehend these arrangements.

As an Amendment to Mr Peter Hardy's proposed Motion (Fossil Fuel Levy Regulations):

Mr Rhodri Morgan
Mr Paul Flynn

and further notes that the omission of the parenthesis inside the large bracket before the $D_{\hat{y}}$ -1 term could lead to the possibility of confusion amongst electricity companies and their consumers as to exactly how much nuclear power they are required to buy.

⊰ HEAR, HEAR! ⊱

Usually pronounced '*yer, yer*', this is the normal way of expressing approval in the Commons Chamber (and in the Lords). Clapping is very unusual, but the Chamber has burst into applause in recent times, as upon the election of Betty Boothroyd as Speaker in 1992, after Tony Blair's last Prime Minister's Question Time in 2007 and on the election of John Bercow as Speaker in 2009.

Erskine May **says** that Members must not disturb a Member who is speaking by hissing, chanting, clapping, booing, exclamations or other interruption, and quotes the Resolution of the House of Commons of 22 January 1693:

> *That Mr Speaker do call upon the Member by name, making such disturbance, and that every such person shall incur the displeasure and censure of the House.*

May **also notes** that:

> *On 19th March 1872 . . . notice was taken of the crowing of cocks, and other disorderly noises, proceeding from Members, principally behind the Chair; and the Speaker condemned them as gross violations of the orders of the House and expressed the pain with which he had heard them.*

◄ EATING IN THE HOUSE ►

From Hansard (13 December 1978):

> Mr J. Enoch Powell (Down, South): *On a point of order, Mr Speaker. Is it possible to ascertain the nature of the objects which the hon. Member for Bolsover (Mr Skinner) is eating, and of which he appears to have a large quantity still available, in order that it may be determined whether they are included amongst the substances which it is permissible to eat in the House?*

Mr Speaker: *Order. I remember in my early days in this House that an hon. Member was unwise enough to try to eat an orange in the Chamber and was pulled up on a point of order. What we must show is courtesy and good manners to each other, which I am quite sure we shall receive.*

***Erskine May* confirms sternly** that no *refreshment* may *be brought into, or consumed in, the Chamber*.

⚜ SNUFF ⚜

But **snuff** is available to Members and Officers of the House from the Principal Doorkeeper. A box, made from the woodwork of the Chamber destroyed in 1941, is kept by the outer door to the Chamber (the one which is slammed in Black Rod's face). It does not need replenishing as often as it once did.

The provision of snuff may have its origin in the prohibition on smoking. In 1693 the House ordered:

That no Member do presume to take tobacco in the gallery of the House.

That no Member do presume to take tobacco at the Table, sitting at Committees.

This rule was for many years relaxed in select committees when they were deliberating in private; but this declined as smoking became less popular. Although the two Houses were not covered by the prohibition on smoking in a public place introduced by the Health Act 2006, they observe it voluntarily, and on 1 July 2007 the Palace of Westminster and the other parliamentary buildings became no-smoking zones.

⊰ THE AVERAGE LENGTH OF SERVICE ⊱

The average length of time served by MPs, as at February 2009, was 13.4 years.

⊰ THE DUTY OF A MEMBER OF PARLIAMENT ⊱

The duty of an MP to be a representative but not a delegate was classically stated by Edmund Burke in his speech to the electors of Bristol in 1774:

> *It ought to be the happiness and glory of a representative to live in the strictest union, the closest correspondence, and the most unreserved communication with his constituents. Their wishes ought to have great weight with him; their opinion, high respect; their business, unremitted attention. It is his duty to sacrifice his repose, his pleasures, his satisfactions to theirs – and*

above all, ever, and in all cases to prefer their interest to his own. But his unbiased opinion, his mature judgement, his enlightened conscience, he ought not to sacrifice to you, to any man, or to any set of men living . . . Your representative owes you, not his industry only, but his judgement; and he betrays, instead of serving you, if he sacrifices it to your opinion.

⊰ 'NAMING' A MEMBER ⊱

An MP may be 'named' by the Speaker or Deputy Speakers for 'grossly disorderly conduct', 'disregarding the authority of the Chair' or for 'persistently or wilfully obstructing the business of the House by disregarding the rules of the House, or otherwise'.

As soon as a Member is named, the senior Minister present moves a motion 'That Mr . . . be suspended from the service of the House', which must be decided immediately, without debate. If the motion is agreed to, the Member is suspended – for five days on the first occasion, for 20 days for a further offence; and, for the third, for the remainder of the parliamentary session (which will probably be in the next November). If force is required to remove the MP, then the suspension for the remainder of the session automatically comes into force, whether it is the first or second offence.

A Member who is suspended must leave the parliamentary precincts immediately, and he or she receives no parliamentary salary during the suspension.

Members named by the Chair since 1945 include: Dame Irene Ward, Bessie Braddock, Tam Dalyell (on four occasions), Ken Livingstone, Dennis Skinner (on three occasions), Ian Paisley, George Galloway and Alex Salmond.

Those who criticise the modern House of Commons as unruly might reflect on the scenes in February 1881 when Gladstone's administration was attempting to legislate for the protection of persons and property in Ireland. The scene on 3 February (after two MPs had already been named) was described thus by a Member who was present:

All that happened thereafter was an incoherent medley. Mr A. M. Sullivan spoke amid vehement clamour against the Speaker, who explained that he had named Mr Dillon not for interrupting Mr Gladstone on a call to order, but for remaining on his feet when the Speaker rose. Mr Gladstone now made a further effort to go on with his speech, and was at once interrupted by The O'Donoghue, who loudly moved the adjournment of the House. The Speaker taking no notice of this, Mr Parnell jumped up and called out that he moved that Mr Gladstone be no longer heard. Amid stentorian cheers from his own party and indignant shouts from the rest of the House, Mr Parnell reiterated his motion in defiance of the warning of the Speaker, and was immediately named. Mr Gladstone again made the motion for expulsion, which was carried by a majority of 405 to 7, the Irish Members refusing to leave their seats and vote . . .

When Mr Finigan had been removed from the House after the same fashion as Mr Dillon and Mr Parnell, the Speaker called the attention of the House to the conduct of the Irish Members and named them at once. There were twenty-eight of them in all. Mr Gladstone immediately rose and moved for their suspension in a body, and the motion was carried by 410 to 6.

. . . Then came a strange scene, which had never been witnessed in the House of Commons before. The name of each Member was read out in turn by the Speaker, as he called upon him to withdraw. Each Member called upon answered to his name with a short speech condemning the action of the Government, and refusing to go unless removed by superior force. To each Member making such announcement, the Serjeant at Arms advanced and touched him solemnly on the shoulder. In most cases the Member touched at once rose and walked out; one or two exceptionally stalwart Members, however, refused to go until the Serjeant at Arms approached them with such a muster of attendants as made it evident that he commanded sufficient force to compel withdrawal.

Justin Huntly McCarthy, MP (1830–1912)

⊸ APOCRYPHA ⊷

Job description for the Clerk of a Select Committee:
Committee of MPs seeks thwarted academic, capable of being decisive – in different directions and on the same day if necessary. Should be of resilient character, capable of reconciling the irreconcilable. Should exhibit judgement when confronted with insanity, and undoubted, but well-hidden, powers of intellect and persuasion. Ability to produce the appearance of order and procedural rectitude out of complete chaos desirable.

⊸ THE CASTING VOTE ⊷

If on a division in the Commons the numbers are equal, the matter cannot be left as a tie; a decision must be made, and the occupant of the Chair (the Speaker or one of his Deputies) must give a casting vote. In former times the Speaker used to vote according to his own preference, but since the end of the 18th century casting votes are given according to three principles:

1. **The Speaker should always vote for further discussion** so that if the votes are equal on the second reading of a bill, the Speaker votes 'Aye', so that the Bill can be considered in committee, and a final decision taken on third reading.
2. **When no further discussion is possible**, the decision should not be taken except by a majority. If there

were a casting vote on the third reading of a bill, this would be a vote on whether the Bill passed, and the Speaker would vote 'No'. If there had been a tie on the motion of no confidence on 28 March 1979, when the Callaghan Government fell by 311 to 310, the Speaker would have voted 'No' on the grounds that the decision should be that of the majority in the House, and not of the casting vote of the Chair.

3. **On an amendment** the casting vote should be to keep a bill in its existing form.

In the Lords, the ancient rule was that if there were no majority the matter was decided against, and this continues, with the exception that a tie on a stage of a Bill (for example, the third reading) is decided in favour of the bill.

'The Division in the House of Commons on the Irish Home Rule Question: the Ayes, 311; the Noes, 341,' 1886

⚔ SPONTANEITY ⚔

William Joynson-Hicks (later Sir William, later still Viscount Brentford) was born plain William Hicks. He married an heiress, Grace Joynson, and hyphenated her name with his. Joynson-Hicks was an adamant opponent of Lloyd George's radical Budgets. In one there was a proposal to tax 'unearned increments'. Joynson-Hicks interrupted Lloyd George at the Despatch Box with: *Will the right honourable Gentleman tell us what is meant by 'unearned increment'.* LG responded with: *On the spur of the moment I can think of no better example of an unearned increment than the hyphen in the honourable Gentleman's name.*

From Hansard (11 November 1947):

Mr Churchill: *Here I see the hand of the master craftsman, the Lord President.*

Mr Herbert Morrison: The *right honourable Gentleman has promoted me.*

Mr Churchill: *Craft is common both to skill and deceit.*

From Hansard (27 April 1961):

Mr Macmillan: *I have never been Home Secretary or Minister of Education. Therefore my experience has been entirely on the receiving end of the matter.*

Mr Emrys Hughes: *Look at the result.*

Mr Macmillan: *Judged by certain aspects, that might be said to be not altogether unsuccessful.*

⚔ SLEEP ⚔

Lord North would feign sleep during speeches by opponents. One exclaimed, during a fevered attack upon the Government: *Even now, in the midst of these perils, the noble Lord is asleep.* North responded: *I wish to God I was.*

Late at night in committee on a Finance Bill in the 1966 Parliament, Harold Lever, then Financial Secretary to the Treasury, closed his eyes briefly during the moving of an amendment by his Opposition counterpart, who immediately accused him of slumber. Lever rose and said: *The honourable Gentleman may no more assume that, because my eyes are closed, I am asleep, than I may assume that, because his eyes are open, he is awake,* sat down, and closed his eyes again.

Lever was sometimes attacked on the grounds that his great personal wealth was at odds with his Labour principles. He would say simply: *I was a socialist before I was a millionaire.*

⚔ THE SPECIAL RELATIONSHIP ⚔

Thomas Jefferson was the principal author of the Declaration of Independence, and the third President of the United States, serving for two terms. As Vice-President (and so President of the United States Senate) between 1797 and 1801 he prepared a *Manual of Parliamentary Practice*. Although it was written for his own guidance, it was also influential in the development of procedure and practice in the US Congress.

Jefferson began by quoting Speaker Arthur Onslow, often accounted the first impartial Speaker of the Commons, who held the office from 1727 to 1761. Jefferson's principal source was the *Precedents of Proceedings* of John Hatsell, Clerk of the Commons from 1768 to 1820, and he quoted from the procedural writings of Henry Elsynge (Clerk of the House 1640–1649), Henry Scobell (Clerk of the House 1649–1658) and John Rushworth, who was Clerk Assistant when the King came to arrest the Five Members in 1642. Jefferson quoted Speaker Onslow as saying:

> *Nothing tended to throw more power into the hands of administration and those who acted with a majority of the House of Commons than a neglect of or departure from the rules of proceeding; that these forms, as instituted by our ancestors, operated as a check and control on the actions of the majority, and that they were, in many instances, a shelter and protection to the minority, against the attempts of power.*

V

PARLIAMENT AT WAR

Air raid warning: sitting suspended.

⚔ BLOOD, TOIL, TEARS AND SWEAT ⚔

On Monday 13 May 1940, just before three o'clock in the afternoon, Winston Churchill ended his first speech to the House of Commons as Prime Minister thus:

In this crisis I hope I may be pardoned if I do not address the House at any length today. I hope that any of my friends and colleagues, and former colleagues, who are affected by the political reconstruction, will make allowance, all allowance, for any lack of ceremony with which it has been necessary to act [in the rapid formation of a coalition Government]. *I would say to the House, as I have said to those who have joined this Government: 'I have nothing to offer but blood, toil, tears and sweat.'*

We have before us an ordeal of the most grievous kind. We have before us many, many long months of struggle and of suffering. You ask, what is our policy? It is to wage war, by sea, land and air, with all our might and with all the strength that God can give us; to wage war against a monstrous tyranny, never surpassed in the dark, lamentable catalogue of human crime. That is our policy. You ask, what is our aim? I can answer in one word: it is victory, victory at all costs, victory in spite of all terror, victory, however long and hard the road may be; for without victory there is no survival. Let that be realised; no survival for the British Empire, no survival for all that the British Empire has stood for, no survival for the urge and impulse of the ages, that mankind will move forward towards its goal. But I take up my task with buoyancy and hope. I feel sure that our cause will not be suffered to fail among men. At this time I feel entitled to claim the aid of all, and I say: 'Come then, let us go forward together with our united strength.'

⚔ AIR RAID WARNINGS ⚔

On receipt of an air raid warning Members are requested to make their way immediately to the nearest refuge, as indicated by direction arrows on the notices posted in the corridors. These refuges are in various parts of the building. If the House is sitting when an air raid warning is received, the Speaker (or Chairman) will at once announce 'Air raid warning – sitting suspended'.

Air raid warnings will be made known by Police and Custodians who, in addition to calling out 'Air raid warning', will blow sharp blasts on their whistles.

Charles Howard, Serjeant at Arms (1939)

⊰ A LETTER TO THE SPEAKER ⊱

Sir, beinge commanded by you to this service, I thinke my selfe bound to acquaint you with the good hand of God towards you and us. Wee marched yesterday after the King, whoe went before us from Daventree to Haverbrowe, and quartered about six miles from him. Hee drew out to meet us; both Armies engaged; wee after 3 howers fight . . . att last routed his Armie, killed and took about 5000 . . . Wee tooke also about 200 carrages, all hee had, and all his guns . . .

Sir, this is non other but the hand of God, and to him aloane belongs the Glorie, wherin non are to share with him . . . Honest men served you faithfully in this action. Sir, they are trustye; I beseech you in the name of God not to discorage them. I wish this action may beget thankfulnesse and humility in all that are concerned in itt . . .

In this Hee rests whoe is
Your most humble servant,
Oliver Cromwell

The letter was written in the evening of 14 June 1645. That day King Charles I was defeated at the Battle of Naseby, near Market Harborough, by a Parliamentary army under Sir Thomas Fairfax. Cromwell commanded the right wing. William Lenthall was the Speaker of the House of Commons, and in 1642 it had been he who asserted the independence of the House when Charles had entered the Chamber with armed men to arrest the five Members.

⚔ THE KING TRIES TO ARREST ⚔
THE FIVE MEMBERS

The 'Five Members' ('who were they?' is a useful quiz question; the answer is Hampden, Haslerigg, Holles, Pym and Strode) had been accused by the King of treason.

Soldiers surrounded the House, and the King came into the Chamber. John Rushworth, the Clerk Assistant, calmly noted down the King's words (the King saw that he was doing so, and later sent for the note, returning it with corrections):

Gentlemen, said the King in halting sentences, I am sorry of this occasion of coming unto you. Yesterday I sent a Serjeant at Arms upon a very important occasion to apprehend some that by my command were accused of high treason; whereunto I did expect obedience and not a message. And I must declare to you here, that albeit no King that ever was in England shall be more careful of your privileges to maintain them to the uttermost of this power than I shall be; yet you must know that in cases of treason no person hath a privilege. And, therefore, I am come to know if any of these persons that were accused were here.

Then casting his eyes upon all the Members in the House, he said: I do not see any of them; I think I should know them. For I must tell you, gentlemen, that so long as these persons that are accused (for no slight crime, but for treason) are here, I cannot expect that the House will be in the right way that I do heartily wish it.

Therefore I am come to tell you, that I must have them, wheresoever I find them.

Then His Majesty said: Is Mr Pym here? to which nobody gave answer. Well, since I see all my birds are flown, I do expect from you that you shall send them unto me as soon as they return hither . . .

When the King asked where the five were, Speaker Lenthall replied:

May it please Your Majesty, I have neither ears to see nor tongue to speak in this place, save as this House doth direct me.

Speaker Lenthall asserts the privileges of the Commons to Charles I, 1642

This was an act of considerable courage and – fortunately for Lenthall's reputation – it is the thing for which he is remembered. But he was a poor Speaker and the rest of his career – once described as 'a strange mixture of fearfulness and indecision' was no ornament to Parliament. In 1648 he was in the Chair and put the Question that the King should be tried; and on his deathbed in 1662 said:

> *I confess with Saul; I held their clothes while they murdered him; but herein I was not so criminal as Saul, for I never consented to his death. No excuse can be made for me, that I proposed the bloody Question for trying the King; but I hoped even then when I put the Question, the very putting the Question would have cleared him, because I believed they were four to one against it – Cromwell and his agents deceived me.*

⊰ THE OUTBREAK OF ⊱
THE FIRST WORLD WAR

Towards the end of the brilliant, cloudless summer of 1914 it became clear that war was imminent. No amount of desperate diplomatic effort could stop the slide into mobilisation and the catastrophe of the First World War.

On the afternoon of Monday 3 August, the Foreign Secretary, Sir Edward Grey, rose to speak in the House of Commons:

> *Last week I stated that we were working for peace not*

only for this country but to preserve the peace of Europe. Today events move so rapidly that it is exceedingly difficult to state with technical accuracy the actual state of affairs, but it is clear that the peace of Europe cannot be preserved. Russia and Germany, at any rate, have declared war upon each other . . .

Towards the end of a lengthy speech, in which he traced the history of the Treaty of 1870 in which Great Britain had guaranteed the neutrality of Belgium (with copious quotation from Mr Gladstone), he said:

Shortly before I reached the House I was informed that the following telegram had been received from the King of the Belgians by our King – King George:

'Remembering the numerous proofs of Your Majesty's friendship, and the friendly attitude of England in 1870, and the proof of friendship she has just given us again, I make a supreme appeal to the diplomatic intervention of you Majesty's Government to safeguard the integrity of Belgium.'

. . . The most awful responsibility is resting upon the Government in deciding what to advise the House of Commons to do. We have disclosed our mind to the House of Commons. We have disclosed the issue, the information which we have, and made clear to the House, I trust, that we are prepared to face that situation, and that, should it develop, as probably it may develop, we shall face it. We have worked for peace up to the last moment, and beyond the last moment.

But that is over, as far as the peace of Europe is

concerned . . . . I believe, when the country realises what is at stake, what the real issues are, the magnitude of the impending dangers in the West of Europe which I have endeavoured to describe to the House, we shall be supported throughout, not only by the House of Commons, but by the determination, the resolution, the courage, and the endurance of the whole country.

Later that evening, Grey rose to inform the House that Germany had sent a note to the Belgian Government seeking free passage of her forces across Belgium. The British Government sent an ultimatum to the German Government seeking assurances about Belgian neutrality. In conversation afterwards, Grey was heard to say: *I hate war*. ***I hate war.*** As dusk was falling, Grey returned to the Foreign Office. He recalled:

We were standing at a window of my room. It was getting dusk, and the lamps were being lit in the space below on which we were looking. I remarked on this with the words: 'The lamps are going out all over Europe; we shall not see them lit again in our lifetime.'

Later still on the evening of 3 August:

. . . some of us sat with the Prime Minister [Asquith] in the Cabinet Room in 10 Downing Street. I was there in touch with the Foreign Office to certify that no satisfactory reply had come from Berlin, though this was, after all that had happened, a foregone conclusion and a matter of form. Churchill also was among those

present, ready at the appointed hour to send out the war order that the Fleet were expecting. Midnight came. We were at war.

⊨ STRATFORD-ON-AVON ⊨

This was to be Parliament's destination if it were to be evacuated from London during the Second World War.

Sir Bernard Coode, Clerk of Public Bills, in 1945:
> *Before war broke out in 1939, a plan had been evolved for the evacuation of Parliament to another place, which was kept secret. Billets for Members of both Houses were settled, transport, which involved in some cases railheads to which parties were to be conducted, were detailed. A certain amount of office baggage was kept packed in readiness for any emergency.*

The secrecy was evidently effective. **A.P. Herbert** remembered *receiving a mysterious packet of secret instructions and labels. No destination was named, and I have no notion where we were to go.*

Hugh Farmer, a Senior Clerk, led reconnaissances to Stratford in 1940:
> *We were given lists of houses in practically every road in Stratford and some better ones outside. We spent*

days trudging up and down inspecting every house. They were worthy two and three bedroom houses, but pretty small rooms. We quickly came to the decision that Members could be made to sleep in double rooms, but not in double beds.

Members of the House of Lords, by contrast, were to be put up in the Falcon Hotel and the Shakespeare Hotel.

But because **the King and Queen were determined** not to leave London, it quickly became clear that there was no chance of Parliament leaving either.

⚜ BOMBS AT WESTMINSTER ⚜

In 1885 the Fenians (a group opposed to a British presence in Ireland) planted a **bomb** at the foot of the staircase leading down from Westminster Hall to the Crypt Chapel. The bomb was discovered and carried out into Westminster Hall by a daring policeman. It exploded, blowing out the great east window and making a large hole in the floor.

Between 1939 and 1945 the Palace of Westminster was hit in **14 air raids** (including one on 26 September in which a bomb blew out the great east window of Westminster Hall again).

On the night of 10 May 1941 the Palace was hit 12 times, and the Commons Chamber was completely destroyed. A few days later, on 16 May 1941, Harold Nicolson described the scene:

> *I go to see the ruins of the old Chamber. It is impossible to get through the Members' Lobby which is a mass of twisted girders. So I went up by the staircase to the Ladies' Gallery and then suddenly, when I turned the corridor there was the open air and a sort of Tintern Abbey gaping before me. The little Ministers' rooms to right and left of the Speaker's Lobby were still intact, but from there onwards there was absolutely nothing. No sign of anything but <u>murs calcinés</u> and twisted girders.*

The official fire brigade report described the event in more bureaucratic style:

> <u>*House of Commons*</u>*: A building of two floors about 100 x 60 feet (used as Assembly Hall and offices) and contents severely damaged by fire, most part of roof off.*

On 17 June 1974 a 20-pound (9-kilogram) **bomb** planted by the Provisional IRA exploded at the north end of Westminster Hall; and on 30 March 1979 a **car bomb** killed Airey Neave, Shadow Secretary of State for Northern Ireland, as he drove out of the underground car park.

⊰ VIOLENT ENDS ⊱

One Speaker, William Tresham, who was Speaker four times in the 1440s, was **murdered** in 1450.

Sir John Wenlock, Speaker 1455–1456, was **killed** at the Battle of Tewkesbury in 1471.

Seven former Speakers of the Commons were **executed**:
   Sir John Bussy, Speaker 1393–1394, beheaded in 1399
   Thomas Thorpe, Speaker 1453–1454, beheaded in 1461
   Thomas Tresham, Speaker in 1459, beheaded in 1471
   William Catesby, Speaker in 1484, beheaded after the Battle of Bosworth in 1485
   Two ex-Speakers, Sir Richard Empson (Speaker 1491–1492) and Edmond Dudley (Speaker in 1504) were beheaded together on the same day in 1510
   . . . and the most famous of them all, Sir Thomas More, who was Speaker in the summer of 1523, was, as Lord Chancellor, beheaded in 1535.

But the last Clerk (although not Clerk of the House) to be **executed** was much more recent: Erskine Childers in 1922. Childers served in the House from 1894 to his resignation in 1910, mostly as Clerk of various select committees, with a period of leave of absence to fight in the Boer War in 1900. He is best remembered as the author of one of the first great spy novels, *The Riddle of the Sands*, published in

1903, in which two Englishmen on a sailing holiday around the treacherous waters and sandbanks of the Friesian Islands discover the Germans rehearsing plans for an invasion. The book caught the national mood of the time and became an immediate bestseller.

He fought in the First World War, ending the war as a Lieutenant-Commander RNVR with the Distinguished Service Cross. Immersing himself in Irish politics, he rejected the dominion status of the Free State in favour of total independence, and he joined the Irish Republican Army, becoming regarded as a traitor by both the Free State and the British. He was arrested on 10 November 1922 (refusing to open fire in case non-combatants were injured) and was shot by a Free State firing party at Beggar's Bush Barracks, Dublin, on 24 November. On the morning of his death he wrote a note to his wife:

It is 6 a.m. You will be pleased to see how imperturbable I have been this night and a.m. It all seems perfectly simple and inevitable, like lying down after a long day's work.

As he entered the courtyard in which he was to be shot, he said:

I am at peace with the world. I bear no grudge against anyone and trust no-one bears any against me.

He shook hands with each member of the firing squad, and as they took up their positions said: *Come closer, boys. It will be easier for you.*

⚜ SECRET SESSIONS ⚜

Between 1940 and 1944 the House of Commons sat in secret **62** times.

The House met in secret session during the war for one reason – and for one reason only – to keep from the enemy information which might help him in the prosecution of the war.

Herbert Morrison

Over the same period the House of Lords sat in secret **58** times.

Both Houses also sat in secret during the First World War.

VI

PRIME MINISTER AND FIRST LORD OF THE TREASURY

Above any other position of eminence, that of Prime Minister is filled by fluke.

Enoch Powell

Bernard Woolley: *I think the Prime Minister wants to govern Britain.*
Sir Humphrey Appleby: *Well stop him, Bernard!*
From the TV series *Yes, Minister*

⊰ PRIME MINISTERS ⊱

There have been **52** including Sir Robert Walpole (the first) and Gordon Brown.

16 were born in London, **seven** in Scotland, **two** (Wellington and Shelburne) in Ireland and **one** (Bonar Law) in Canada.

Two (MacDonald and Baldwin) were an only child. The PM with the most siblings was **Sir Robert Walpole**, who had nine brothers and seven sisters.

Wednesday 28th March 1979

Ipswich Port Authority Bill, — read 3° & passed

Shetland Islands Council Order Confirmation Bill,—
Lerwick Harbour Order Confirmation Bill,—
Gairloch Pier Order Confirmation Bill,—

consid: deferred till T°

Accepted, Papers

Mr Peter Viggers   *Ordered*

SERVICES WIDOWS (PROVISION OF PENSIONS),—That leave be given to bring in a Bill
to make further provision for service pensions and in particular to provide pensions for
widows of non-commissioned servicemen who retired before 1st September 1950 *& that*

et al. do prepare & bring it in.

Services Widows (Provision of Pensions),— Mr Peter Viggers
accordingly presented a Bill to . . . : And an same was
read 1° & ordered to be read 2° upon Friday 30th March.

NO CONFIDENCE IN HER MAJESTY'S GOVERNMENT,—

Mrs Margaret Thatcher
~~Mr William Whitelaw~~
~~Sir Keith Joseph~~
~~Sir Geoffrey Howe~~
~~Mr James Prior~~
~~Mr Francis Pym~~

Motion made & Question put,

That this House has no confidence in Her Majesty's Government.

The House divided :

Ayes		Noes	
311	Mr Spencer Le Marchant	Mr James Hamilton	310
	Mr Michael Roberts	Mr Donald Coleman	

Resolved etc . . . .

EXPENDITURE,—   *Ordered,*

Mr Walter Harrison

That the Standing Order of 18th November 1974 relating to the nomination of the
Expenditure Committee be amended, by leaving out Mr Philip Goodhart and inserting
Mr David Atkinson.

Adjournment, — Resolved, That this House do
now adjourn (Mr Peter Snape).

Adjourned accordingly at
10.42 pm

The fall of the Callaghan Government, 28 March 1979, recorded in the Minute
Book of the House by the Clerk at the Table (later Clerk of the House), Sir
Kenneth Bradshaw.

Henry VIII on the throne at the State Opening of Parliament in 1523.

Die Martis 12° February 1688

The Declaration of the Lords Spirituall
Temporall and Comons Assembled at Westm

Whereas the late King James the second by the
assistance of diverse evill Councellors Judges and
Ministers imployed by him did endeavour to
subvert and extirpate the Protestant Religion
and the Lawes and Libertyes of this Kingdome.

By assumeing and exerciseing a Power of dis-
pencing and suspending of Lawes and the execution
of Lawes without consent of Parliament:

By committing and prosecuteing diverse worthy
Prelates for humbly petitioning to be excused from
concurring to the said assumed Power

By issueing a Commission under the Great Seale
for erecting a Court called the Comissioners for
Ecclesiasticall Causes

By levying money for and to the use of the Crowne
by pretence of Prerogative for other time and in
other manner then the same was granted by Parliament.

By raiseing and keeping a standing Army within
this Kingdom in time of Peace without consent of
Parliament, and quartering souldiers contrary to Law

By causeing severall good subjects being
Protestants to be disarmed at the same time when
Papists were both armed and imployed
By violateing the freedome of
members to serve in Parliament

By causeing
and prosecuted in the
for matters and causes
and by divers other
illegall courses. By Prosecutions
of Kings Bench for matters
cognicable only in Parliament did by divers
other Arbitrary & illegall

The draft Declaration of Rights of 1688, which became the Bill of Rights later that year. The ink blot was probably made by the Clerk at the Table during the debate.

The House of Commons sitting in 1808, Speaker Abbot in the Chair, by A. C. Pugin and Thomas Rowlandson. The chandelier 'at the branch' is at the top of the picture (see page 9).

George IV's Coronation Banquet, 19 July 1821: The Bringing up of the First Course, by Charles Wild.

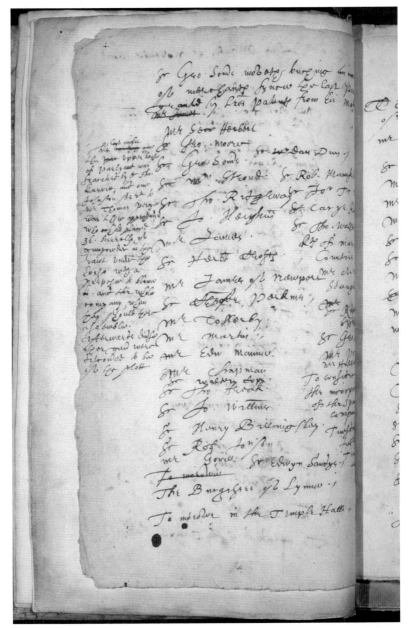

The Gunpowder Journal, 5 November 1605. The discovery of the Plot is recorded in a marginal note by the Clerk of the House, Ralph Ewens.

The Trial of Warren Hastings before the House of Lords in Westminster Hall, 1788.

The first page of the Act of Union between England and Scotland, 1707.

The Dynamite Explosions at the Houses of Parliament, from *The Graphic* newspaper, 31 January 1885.

29 had an MP as a father. **18** were Old Etonians.

13 Prime Ministers went to Christ Church, Oxford.

Four (Wilmington, Pitt the Younger, Balfour and Heath) never married.

The Prime Minister with the most children was Grey (**17**).

'Yes, I have climbed to the top of the greasy pole' – *Disraeli on becoming Prime Minister, 1868,* Punch

The oldest when he became Prime Minister was Palmerston (71); the youngest was Pitt the Younger (24 years 205 days).

The longest period in office was Walpole's (20 years 314 days). The longest periods of office starting in the last century were those of Margaret Thatcher (11 years 209 days) and Tony Blair (10 years 55 days).

The longest periods of office starting in the 19th century were Liverpool (14 years 305 days), Salisbury (13 years 252 days) and Gladstone (12 years 126 days).

The shortest periods of office were those of Canning (119 days), Goderich (130 days), Bonar Law (209 days), Devonshire (225 days), Shelburne (266 days), Bute (317 days) and Douglas-Home (363 days).

The oldest at their deaths were Callaghan, Douglas-Home and Macmillan, all of whom lived to be 92. The youngest were Devonshire (44) and Pitt the Younger (46).

◄ PRIME MINISTERS ON PRIME MINISTERS ►

Harold Macmillan on Harold Wilson's claim of youthful poverty:

> *If Harold Wilson ever went to school without any boots, it can only have been that he was too big for them.*

Harold Wilson on Harold Macmillan:

> *He has inherited the streak of charlatanry in Disraeli without his vision, and the self-righteousness of Gladstone without his dedication to principle.*

David Lloyd George on Neville Chamberlain:
He saw foreign policy through the wrong end of a municipal drainpipe. He might make an adequate Lord Mayor of Birmingham in a bad year.

Lord Derby on W.E. Gladstone:
Gladstone's jokes are no laughing matter.

Benjamin Disraeli on Sir Robert Peel:
A burglar of other intellects; there is no other statesman who has committed political larceny on such a grand scale.

Benjamin Disraeli on W.E. Gladstone, in a letter to Lord Derby:
That unprincipled maniac Gladstone – extraordinary mixture of envy, vindictiveness, hypocrisy and superstition.
And on another occasion:
He has not a single redeeming defect.

W.E. Gladstone on Disraeli:
The Tory Party had principles by which it would and did stand for bad and for good. All this Dizzy destroyed.

Lord Grenville, a political colleague of Gladstone's, wrote to Queen Victoria after Disraeli had lost the 1880 Election:
Lord Beaconsfield [Disraeli] and Mr Gladstone are men of extraordinary ability; they dislike each other more than is usual among public men. Of no other politician Lord Beaconsfield would have said in public that his conduct

was worse than those who committed the Bulgarian atrocities. He has the power of saying in two words that which drives a person of Mr Gladstone's peculiar temperament into a state of great excitement.

Disraeli on Gladstone again:

A sophistical rhetorician, inebriated with the exuberance of his own verbosity, and gifted with an egotistical imagination that can at all times command an interminable and inconsistent series of arguments to malign an opponent and glorify himself.

And, when Disraeli was asked to explain the difference between a misfortune and a calamity:

If Mr Gladstone fell into the Serpentine that would be a misfortune. But if someone were to pull him out again, that would be a calamity.

Churchill on Attlee:

A modest man, with much to be modest about.

Attlee on Churchill:

*Fifty per cent of Winston is genius, fifty per cent bloody fool. He **will** behave like a child.*

Neville Chamberlain on Arthur Balfour:

He always seemed to me to have a heart of stone.

The Duke of Wellington on Sir Robert Peel:

I have no small-talk and Peel has no manners.

Disraeli on Sir Robert Peel:
> *The right honourable Gentleman's smile is like the silver fittings on a coffin.*

Harold Wilson:
> *The main essentials of a Prime Minister are sleep and a sense of history.*

⊰ THE IRISH QUESTION ⊱

Sellar and Yeatman, *1066 And All That*:
> [Gladstone] *spent his declining years trying to guess the answer to the Irish Question; unfortunately, when he was getting warm, the Irish secretly changed the Question.*

Benjamin Disraeli:
> *Ah, Ireland . . . That damnable, delightful country, where everything that is right is the opposite of what it ought to be . . .*

⊰ LUVVIES ⊱

There is no **jealousy** as great as artistic jealousy. Lord John Russell published a novel, *The Nun of Arronca*, and a five-act play in blank verse, *Don Carlos*.

Of the first, **Benjamin Disraeli** said:
> *The feeblest romance in our literature.*

And of the second:
> *The feeblest tragedy in our language.*

Disraeli also said:
> *An author who speaks about his own books is almost as bad as a mother who talks about her own children . . .*

⊰ THE ONLY BRITISH PRIME MINISTER ⊱ TO BE ASSASSINATED

The victim was Spencer Perceval on 11 May 1812. A Commons Committee was examining the effects on trade of Orders in Council aimed at damaging French commerce, and complained that the Prime Minister was not present. Perceval was sent for. On his way he passed through the Lobby of the House of Commons, where he was shot by John Bellingham. While trading in Russia, Bellingham had suffered losses at the hands of the Russians and bitterly resented the lack of assistance he had received from the British Ambassador and then from the British Government. This became something of an obsession: Bellingham petitioned everyone in sight for redress – including Perceval, who refused to intervene.

Bellingham was hanged a week later after his plea of insanity was rejected at the Old Bailey.

The assassination of Spencer Perceval, 1812

Henry Bellingham, a descendant, was elected MP for North West Norfolk in 2001.

Although the **assassination** was of a Member of the House of Commons, and took place in the House of Commons, the House of Lords seems to have decided to take charge. Its *Journal* for that day reads:

The House being informed, That a most melancholy and atrocious Circumstance had taken place in the Lobby of the Lower House of Parliament;

ORDERED, That the Officers and Attendants of this House do prevent all Persons from quitting this House, or the Passages or Avenues thereto, till this House has made such Examination, touching the said atrocious Circumstance, as shall be satisfactory to this House.

The House continued sitting Half an Hour, and the Yeoman Usher being ordered to go down to the Lower House of Parliament, to enquire if that House were sitting, informed the House, 'That he had been to the House of Commons, in pursuance of their Lordships' Order, and found that that House was adjourned till To-morrow morning.'

⚔ SURVEYOR OF THE MELTINGS AND ⚔ CLERK OF THE IRONS

An appointment at the Royal Mint, requiring the performance of no duties whatsoever, but worth £120 a year [£6,723 in 2009 money], which was held in the 1790s by Spencer Perceval.

⚔ THE FIRST NON-OXBRIDGE-EDUCATED ⚔ PRIME MINISTER

The first university-educated PM who did not go to Oxford or Cambridge was not Gordon Brown, as is often stated, but the Earl of Bute, Prime Minister 1762–1763, who attended the University of Leiden.

◄ THE SMALLEST PRIME MINISTER ►

The smallest PM was almost certainly Lord John Russell, who was 5 feet 4¾ inches (164.5 centimetres) tall and weighed eight stone (50.8 kilograms).

He was born in Westminster, in Hertford Street, on 18 August 1792, the third son of the Duke of Bedford. At elections he would counter criticism of his size by saying that he had been taller, but was *worn away by the anxieties and struggles of the Reform Bill.*

In his youth he travelled extensively in southern Europe and visited Napoleon during the latter's brief exile on Elba. He is supposed to have told Napoleon at some length about his own family; which discourse Napoleon heard in total silence, and at the end went to a corner of the room and relieved himself.

Earl Russell (formerly Lord John Russell); by Ape *(Carlo Pellegrini), 1869*

Sydney Smith said of Russell's studied calmness:

He would perform the operation for the stone, build St Paul's, or assume the command of the Channel Fleet and no-one would discover from his manner that the patient had died, the church tumbled down and the Fleet had been knocked to atoms.

Lord Lytton wrote:

Next, cool and all unconscious of reproach,
Comes the calm of Johnny who upset the coach.

Russell never forgave either of them; he was resentful of any criticism, and of others being credited in his place (especially for the 1832 Reform Bill, which he felt was his alone). He was created Earl Russell in 1861. Frail and often in bad health, he lived to be 85.

⊀ HEIGHT ⊁

Height, or a lack of it, was said to have been the reason why the career of Leo Amery (1873–1955) did not fulfil the expectations of many. It was said of him that he would have been Prime Minister if he had been half a head taller and his speeches half an hour shorter.

⚜ HAROLD MACMILLAN WAS ⚜ THE LAST PRIME MINISTER

. . . to have been **born** in the reign of Queen Victoria.

. . . to have **fought** in the First World War.

. . . to have **had a moustache** (as Prime Minister, that is).

⚜ THE ONLY PRIME MINISTER TO HOLD ⚜ SEANCES IN NUMBER 10 DOWNING STREET

The only PM to hold seances in Number 10 was (so far as we know) Arthur Balfour (1848–1930), Prime Minister 1902–1905. He was a Cabinet Minister for the astonishing total of 37 years.

As a young MP he had nicknames including 'Tiger Lily', 'The Lisping Hawthorn Bird' and one, 'Pretty Fanny', which has not made an easy transition to 21st-century usage.

But when appointed by his uncle Lord Salisbury as Chief Secretary in Ireland, he was known as 'Bloody Balfour'. The phrase 'Bob's your uncle' probably stems from this swift promotion. If Bob (Robert Cecil, Marquess of Salisbury) was your uncle, the thing was settled.

LORD SALISBURY.

'Sketches in Parliament', the Illustrated London News, *1884*

He did not read newspapers: *I have never put myself to the trouble of rummaging through an immense rubbish-heap on the problematical chance of discovering a cigar-end.* But when Frank Harris, the raffish libertine and author, said to him: *The fact is, Mr Balfour, all the faults of our age come from Christianity and journalism.* Balfour responded: *Christianity, of course; but why journalism?*

Balfour was a brilliant performer in the House of Commons, but had a reputation for being somewhat semi-detached. As Foreign Secretary he tried hard not to travel abroad. Churchill said of him: *If you wanted nothing done, Arthur Balfour was the best man for the task. There was no equal to him.*

He had many close women friends but never married. Margot Tennant (who later married Asquith) teased him for his detachment, saying that she was sure that he would not much mind if his closest friends – Lady Elcho, Lady Desborough and she herself – were to die. Balfour reflected for a moment, and replied: *I think I should mind if you all died on the same day.*

VII
INSULT AND ORATORY

There is not a more terrible audience in the world.
Thomas Babington Macaulay, of the
House of Commons

⊰ THE COCKPIT ⊱

The House of Commons can seem a benign and even sleepy place, when the subject for debate is uncontroversial and only a handful of Members are in the Chamber. But throughout its history it has changed swiftly from mood to mood, and a packed Chamber when sparks have caught the political tinder can be a fearsome place for a Minister on the defensive at the Despatch Box, or for an individual MP who finds himself or herself in a minority of one.

Disraeli – a masterful performer in the Chamber – nevertheless thought that it was *the most chilling and nerve-destroying audience in the world.*

These days, an MP's constituents would notice quite swiftly if their MP never said anything, but in former days silent Members were not uncommon. One of the more unusual was 'Single-Speech Hamilton'. William Gerard Hamilton (1729–1796) made a storming maiden speech as the new Member for Peterborough in 1755, which was the talk of the House for years. But he is popularly supposed to have left it at that, despite being an MP for the rest of his life (and a Member of the Irish House of Commons, for Kilebegs, from 1761 to 1768).

The collective judgement, the 'feel' of the House, has long been able to see through its Members. Nigel Nicolson said of his entry into the House in 1952:

It was my first lesson in parliamentary deflation. To come from the concentrated arc-lights, the excitement, the triumph, of an election, to the goal of your ambition, and find that the size of your majority is better known than your name, is an immediate reminder that you are of so little significance that when you die or lose your seat, you will probably be replaced as easily as a broken window-pane . . . It is not only the antiquity of Parliament which cuts a man down to size. It is its terrible power to sum up character and detect fraud.

Nicolson may of course have felt rather resentful on his first acquaintance with the House. He came in at a by-election, and so took the Oath alone in front of a crowded House rather than as one of a long shuffling queue after a general election. As he waited at the Bar for the moment to arrive, a senior Member said to him: *In a few minutes you will walk behind the Speaker's Chair into the obscurity from which you should probably never have emerged.*

⚔ INSULTS ⚔

The art of the **insult** is a treasured part of parliamentary life. Generally, the more elegant – and even subtle – the better. But plain abuse often works as well.

Lord Sandwich to John Wilkes:
> *You will die either on the gallows, or of the pox.*

Wilkes:
> *That must depend on whether I embrace your Lordship's principles or your mistress.*

When the future George IV was Prince Regent, the emphatically non-Royalist Wilkes proposed a toast to the health of the King. A little later the Prince expressed his surprise and asked Wilkes for how long he had been concerned for His Majesty's health. *Since I had the pleasure of Your Royal Highness's acquaintance*, Wilkes replied.

Edmund Burke of MPs barracking him during a rowdy sitting of the House:
> *I could teach a pack of hounds to yelp with more melody and equal comprehension.*

Benjamin Disraeli on Gladstone's Government, April 1872:
> *As I sat opposite the Treasury Bench the ministers reminded me of one of those marine landscapes not very unusual on the coasts of South America. You behold a range of exhausted volcanoes.*

Lord Randolph Churchill on Gladstone:
> *An old man in a hurry.*

Henry Labouchère on Gladstone:
> *I don't object to the Old Man always having the ace of trumps up his sleeve, but merely to his belief that God Almighty put it there.*

Stanley Baldwin about the Members of the House of Commons immediately after the First World War:
> *A lot of hard-faced men who look as if they had done very well out of the War.*

Stanley Baldwin on Lloyd George:
> *He spent his whole life in plastering together the true and the false and therefrom extracting the plausible.*

Margot Asquith on Lloyd George:
> *He could not see a belt without hitting below it.*

Lord Curzon on Baldwin:
> *Not even a public figure. A man of no experience. And of the utmost insignificance.*

Aneurin Bevan of Clement Attlee:
> *He brings to the fierce struggle of politics the tepid enthusiasm of a lazy summer's afternoon at a cricket match.*

Clement Attlee had rather a good rejoinder to his critics:
> *Few thought he was even a starter;*

There were many who thought themselves smarter.
But he ended PM – CH and OM;
An Earl, and a Knight of the Garter.

Aneurin Bevan, on a speech by Churchill:
The mediocrity of his thinking is concealed by the majesty of his language.

Winston Churchill, seeing Sir Stafford Cripps walk past in the House of Commons:
There but for the grace of God goes God.

Nigel Birch, on Harold Wilson's first Labour Government:
The most incompetent Government ever to moisten the front bench.

Edward Heath, refusing to say why he thought that Margaret Thatcher disliked him:
I am not a doctor.

John Major on Neil Kinnock:
Neil Kinnock's speeches go on for so long because he has nothing to say, so he has no way of knowing when he has finished saying it.

Martin Flannery, MP for Sheffield Hillsborough from 1974 to 1992, to a Conservative Member who was irritating him:
You could strut sitting down.

⚔ DISMISSAL ⚔

Oliver Cromwell dismissing the Long Parliament (the Rump Parliament), 20 April 1653:

It is high time for me to put an end to your sitting in this place, which you have dishonoured by your contempt of all virtue, and defiled by your practice of every vice; ye are a factious crew, and enemies to all good government; ye are a pack of mercenary wretches, and would like Esau sell your country for a mess of pottage, and like Judas betray your God for a few pieces of money.

Is there a single virtue now remaining among you? Is there one vice you do not possess? Ye have no more religion than my horse; gold is your God; which of you have not bartered your conscience for bribes? Is there a man amongst you that has the least care for the good of the Commonwealth?

Ye sordid prostitutes, have you not defiled this sacred place, and turned the Lord's temple into a den of thieves, by your immoral principles and wicked practices? Ye are grown intolerably odious to the whole nation; you were deputed here by the people to get grievances redressed, and are yourselves gone! So! Take away that shining bauble there [the Mace], *and lock up the doors. In the name of God, go.*

*'Take away that shining bauble there': Oliver Cromwell dissolving
the Long Parliament*

❧ THE ENGLISHMAN'S HOME ❧
IS HIS CASTLE

William Pitt the Elder, first Earl of Chatham (quoted by
Lord Denning in *Southam v. Smout*, 1964):

> *The poorest man may in his cottage bid defiance to all
> the forces of the Crown. It may be frail – its roof may
> shake – the wind may blow through it – the storm may
> enter – the rain may enter – but the King of England
> cannot enter – all his force dares not cross the threshold
> of the ruined tenement.*

⚔ EDMUND BURKE ACCUSES ⚔
WARREN HASTINGS

Warren Hastings had been Governor (later Governor-General) of Bengal between 1772 and 1785. A ruthless and successful administrator, he did much to turn the East India Company from a trading organisation to a governing power; but when he returned to England (much enriched) he encountered fierce criticism. Edmund Burke (1729–1797) was one of the most brilliant orators of his day, who *felt public questions as passionately as other men feel their private joys or reverses*. He devoted himself to the pursuit of Hastings, inside and outside Parliament.

Burke was instrumental in the impeachment of Hastings (a procedure whereby the Commons lay the charges and the case is tried by the Lords acting as a Court). Burke tried to persuade the Commons to bring a total of 22 charges against Hastings; the House agreed on seven. The trial took place in Westminster Hall (the spot where Hastings stood is marked to this day by a plaque) and lasted on and off *for six years*, from 1788 to 1794 (although the court sat for 'only' 142 days during that time).

The peroration of Burke's opening for the prosecution, on 19 February 1788, shows what he was capable of. In the surroundings of Westminster Hall it must have been unforgettable:

> *Therefore I charge Mr Hastings with having destroyed, for private purposes, the whole system of government . . .*

I charge him with having formed a Committee to be mere instruments and tools, at the enormous expense of £62,000 per annum . . .

I charge him with having robbed those persons of whom he took the bribes.

I charge him with having fraudulently alienated the fortunes of widows . . .

I charge him with having . . . wasted the country, destroyed the landed interest, cruelly harassed the peasants, burnt their houses, seized their crops, tortured and degraded their persons, and destroyed the honour of the whole female race of that country.

My Lords, what is it that we want here to a great act of national justice? Do we want a cause, my Lords? You have the cause of oppressed princes, of undone women of the first rank, of desolated provinces and of wasted kingdoms.

Do you want a criminal, my Lords? When was there so much iniquity laid to the charge of anyone? No, my Lords, you must not look to punish any delinquent in India more . . .

My Lords, is it a prosecutor that you want? You have before you the Commons of Great Britain as prosecutors; and I believe, my Lords, that the sun, in his beneficent progress round the world, does not behold a more glorious sight than of men, separated from a remote people by the material bounds and barriers of nature, united by the bonds of a social and moral community; – all the Commons of England resenting as their own the indignities and cruelties that are offered to all the people of India.

. . . Therefore it is with confidence that, ordered by the Commons, I impeach Warren Hastings, Esquire, of high crimes and misdemeanours.

I impeach him in the name of the Commons of Great Britain, whose parliamentary trust he has betrayed.

I impeach him in the name of all the Commons of Great Britain, whose national character he has dishonoured.

I impeach him in the name of the people of India, whose laws, rights and liberties he has subverted, whose properties he has destroyed, whose country he has laid waste and desolate.

I impeach him in the name of and by virtue of those eternal laws of justice which he has violated.

I impeach him in the name of human nature itself, which he has cruelly outraged, injured and oppressed, in both sexes, in every age, rank, situation and condition of life.

Hastings was – eventually – acquitted of all the charges, but his reputation was irreparably damaged, and he spent the rest of his life in obscurity.

Tom Paine said of Edmund Burke:
As he rose like a rocket, so he fell like a stick.

⊹ THE DOME ⊹

Moving the motion in the House of Lords for an Humble Address to be presented to Her Majesty to thank her for the Queen's Speech, **Lord Falconer of Thoroton**, former Lord Chancellor, said:

> *I was able to achieve what no Minister in government, before or since, has achieved – namely, to have every single national newspaper call for my resignation on the same day. I waited patiently for the storm to pass; 10 days later, the Daily Star started its leader column with the words: 'Lord Falconer should not resign.'*
>
> *It was a Brownesque comeback, you might think – but no; it went on: 'Lord Fatty should be placed on the top of the Dome and they should both be burned to a cinder.'*

Hansard (3 December 2008)

⊹ HOW THINGS CAN CHANGE ⊹
IN POLITICS

Benjamin Disraeli to Joseph Hume, 5 June 1832 (when Disraeli was contesting the Wycombe constituency as a Radical):

> *Accept my sincere, my most cordial thanks . . . Believe me, Sir, that if it be my fortune to be returned in the present instance to a Reformed Parliament, I shall*

> *remember with satisfaction that that return is mainly*
> *attributed to the interest expressed in my success by one*
> *of the most distinguished and able of our citizens.*

But less than four years later, when **Disraeli** had left the Radicals, he said to Hume:

> *You are a man who, having scraped together a fortune*
> *by jobbing in Government contracts in a colony,*
> *and entering the House of Commons as the Tory*
> *representative of a close corporation, became the*
> *apostle of economy and unrestricted suffrage; and you*
> *close a career, commenced and matured in corruption,*
> *by spouting Sedition in Middlesex and counselling*
> *rebellion in Canada.*

12 January 1836

Eliza Savage (d. 1885):

> *I saw Mr Gladstone in the street last night. I waited and*
> *waited but no cab ran over him.*

⊰ A TEN-MINUTE-RULE SPEECH ⊱

In the Commons on Tuesdays and Wednesdays for most of the session Members have the opportunity to seek leave to bring in '**a Ten-Minute Rule Bill**', and can make their case for legislation in a speech of not more than 10 minutes. Ten-Minute Rule Bills rarely become law, but this is an opportunity to trail an idea and to get the House's endorsement. A Member opposing the idea gets 10 minutes in which to do so. There follows a memorable example of a speech against; in this case, as will become clear, a speech against proposed legislation to register chiropodists, on 21 October (Trafalgar Day) 1969. It was made by John (later Sir John) Smith, MP for the Cities of London and Westminster 1965–1970, who was also the founder of the Landmark Trust:

> *I oppose the Motion. I realise that the Bill may well not reach the Statute Book, and I have no wish to inconvenience the honourable Member for Southall (Mr Bidwell), but I do not consider that we should allow it to be introduced. There is a matter of principle here. What I have to say will take only a minute or two, and I do not intend to divide the House.*
>
> *Why are chiropodists to be registered? The real reason is nothing more than that they are not registered already. This will mean a new law, to be studied by many and broken by some. It will mean new offences. It will mean more work for civil servants. It will require inspectors. There will be a small further shove on the downhill road that leads to a country in which everything which is not actually forbidden is compulsory. Do we really want a country in which everyone is organised and lined up like the graves in a war cemetery?*
>
> *Further, is the registration of chiropodists what Parliament is for? It could perfectly well be left entirely to the profession. What are we to say when at the latter day we are called to the dreadful bar of judgement and*

we are asked what we were doing in Parliament, at this colossal juncture in our national affairs, when there is civil unrest in Northern Ireland, and industrial unrest in our own country, when our economy is far from healthy, when society is shaken by arguments and divisions on important moral problems, and when the Russians and the Americans are not registering chiropodists, but are reaching out into space? What are we to say when we are asked what we, the heirs of Trafalgar, were doing in Parliament today, the anniversary of the Battle of Trafalgar? Are we to say, 'Well, actually, we were registering chiropodists'?

This is not a party matter. I appeal to all with any trace of greatness to take their eyes off their feet. Let us leave these chiropodists unregistered. Let us leave just one unregistered corner which is for ever England.

⊣ MORE DISRAELI ⊢

When I want to read a book I write one.

To any aspiring author who sent him a manuscript for perusal:

My dear Mr Snooks,

Thank you so much for sending me the manuscript of your novel. You may be assured that I shall lose no time in reading it.

Yours, &c.

To Lord Palmerston (Prime Minister 1855–1858 and 1859–1865):

> *You owe the Whigs great gratitude, my Lord, and therefore I think that you will betray them. Your Lordship is like a favourite footman on easy terms with his mistress. Your dexterity seems a happy compound of the smartness of an attorney's clerk and the intrigue of a Greek of the lower empire.*

Of Lord John Russell (Prime Minister 1846–1852 and 1865–1866):

> *If a traveller were informed that such a man was Leader of the House of Commons he may begin to comprehend how the Egyptians worshipped an insect.*

> *Damn your principles! Stick to your party!*

Speech in the House of Commons (15 March 1838):

> *The right honourable Gentleman* [Sir Robert Peel] *caught the Whigs bathing, and walked away with their clothes.*

On his deathbed, sitting up and correcting the Hansard proofs of his last speech in the House of Lords:

> *I will **not** go down to posterity speaking bad grammar.*

'He educated the Tories and dished the Whigs to pass Reform; but to
have become what he is from what he was is the greatest reform of all';
Disraeli (Carlo Pellegrini), by Ape, 1869

⚓ O'CONNELL ON DISRAELI ⚓

When it came to invective, Disraeli didn't have it all his
own way. Here is **Daniel O'Connell** at a meeting of trades
unions in Dublin in 1835 – long on insult, short on
subtlety:

> *I must confess there is one of the late attacks on me*
> *which excited in my mind a great deal of astonishment.*
> *(Hear, hear.) It is this: the attack made at Taunton by*
> *Mr Disraeli. In the annals of political turpitude there is*
> *not anything deserving the appellation of political*
> *blackguardism to equal that attack on me. What is my*
> *acquaintance with this man? Just this: in 1831 or the*
> *beginning of 1832, the borough of Wycombe became*
> *vacant. He got an introduction to me, and wrote me a*

letter stating that I was a Radical Reformer, and as he was also a Radical (laughter), and was going to stand upon the Radical interest for the borough of Wycombe where he said there were many persons of that way of thinking who would be influenced by my opinion, he would feel obliged by receiving a letter from me recommendatory of him as a Radical. His letter to me was so distinct upon the subject that I immediately complied with the request, and composed as good a letter as I could in his behalf. Mr Disraeli thought this letter so valuable that he not only took the autograph, but had it printed and placarded. It was, in fact, the ground on which he canvassed the borough. He was, however, defeated, but that was not my fault. (Laughter.) I did not demand gratitude from him, but I think if he had any feeling he would conceive I had done him a civility at least, if not a service, which ought not to be repaid by atrocity of the foulest description. (Cheers.)

The next thing I heard of him was that he had started upon the Radical interest for Marylebone, but was again defeated. Having been twice defeated in the Radical interest, he was just the fellow for the Conservatives (laughter), and accordingly he joined a Conservative club and started for two or three places in the Conservative interest. (Loud laughter.)

At Taunton, this miscreant had the audacity to call me an incendiary! Why, I was a greater incendiary in 1831 than I am at present – if I ever were one (laughter) – and if I am, he is doubly so for having employed me

(Cheers and laughter). Then he calls me a traitor. My answer to that is, that he is a liar (Cheers). He is a liar in action and in words. His life is a living lie. He is a disgrace to his species. What state of society must that be that could tolerate such a creature – having the audacity to come forward with one set of principles at one time, and obtain political assistance by reason of those principles, and at another to profess diametrically the reverse? His life, I say again, is a living lie. He is the most degraded of his species and kind; and England is degraded in tolerating or having on the face of her society a miscreant of his abominable, foul and atrocious nature (Cheers).

Thomas Carlyle described O'Connell as: *A wretched, blustering quack.*

O'Connell constantly complained about the way that he was reported by journalists. On one occasion the excuse of the reporter from *The Times* was that his notebook had got wet in the rain on the way back to the office and had washed the words away. O'Connell said: *That was the most extraordinary shower of rain I ever have heard of. For it not only washed out of your notebook the speech I made, but it also washed in another entirely different one.*

⊰ AMERICAN INDEPENDENCE ⊱

Earl Camden in the House of Lords (1765):

The British Parliament has no right to tax the Americans . . . Taxation and representation are inseparably united. God hath joined them; no British Parliament can put them asunder. To endeavour to do so is to stab our very vitals.

Edmund Burke on American taxation, House of Commons (1774):

Would twenty shillings, have ruined Mr Hampden's fortune? No! but the payment of half twenty shillings, on the principle it was demanded, would have made him a slave.

Edmund Burke, speech on conciliation with America (22 March 1775):

My hold of the colonies is in the close affection which grows from common names, from kindred blood, from similar privileges, and equal protection. These are ties which, though light as air, are as strong as links of iron . . . In no country perhaps in the world is the law so general a study . . . This study renders men acute, inquisitive, dexterous, prompt in attack, ready in defence, full of resources . . . They augur misgovernment at a distance, and sniff the approach of tyranny in every tainted breeze.

❧ CHURCHILL'S LAST GREAT SPEECH ❧

Churchill's last great speech in the House of Commons was probably that on the nuclear deterrent in March 1955. He had said that a quantity of plutonium *less than would fill the Box on the Table* would produce weapons which would give world domination to any great power that had sole possession of the substance. His speech finished:

To conclude: mercifully, there is time and hope if we combine patience and courage. All deterrents will improve and gain authority during the next ten years. By that time, the deterrent may well reach its acme and reap its final reward. The day may dawn when fair play, love for one's fellow-men, respect for justice and freedom, will enable tormented generations to march forth serene and triumphant from the hideous epoch in which we have to dwell. Meanwhile, never flinch, never weary, never despair.

Hansard (1 March 1955)

VIII
THE PEOPLE HAVE SPOKEN

*Every election is a sort of advance auction
sale of stolen goods.*

H.L. Mencken

The people have spoken – the bastards!
Dick Tuck, after losing the 1966 California
State Senate election

⤙ NURSING THE CONSTITUENCY ⤚

For any modern Member of Parliament, the **constituency**
looms very large in his or her life. Its interests and concerns
are rarely off the MP's desk; its constituents provide the
majority of the postbag; and of course those constituents
must be wooed to maximise the chances of re-election. So
the prudent MP will spend time holding 'surgeries' to hear
constituents' problems, ensuring that constituency cases
are effectively dealt with, and that he or she is seen as an
assiduous champion. This takes a lot of hard work and
not a little diplomacy. It was not always so:

Gentlemen,
I received yours and am surprised by your insolence in troubling me about the Excise. You know, what I very well know, that I bought you. And I know, what perhaps you think I don't know, you are now selling yourselves to Somebody Else; and I know, what you do not know, that I am buying another borough. May God's curse light upon you all: may your houses be as open and common to all Excise Officers as your wives and daughters were to me, when I stood for your scoundrell corporation.
Yours, etc.,
Anthony Henley

Henley was Member of Parliament for Southampton from 1727 to 1734, and the elder brother of Robert Henley, afterwards Lord Chancellor and first Earl of Northington. In 1733, the year before this letter was written, he had eloped with Lady Betty Berkeley, a 15-year-old heiress. The letter was in response to complaints from his constituents about the Excise Bill.

⊰ A MANIFESTO ⊱

A *Punch* cartoon of 1872 showed the **Duke of Abercorn** as Disraeli's butler, telling him:
A deputation, Sir, downstairs, want to know the Conservative programme.

Eh? Oh! Ah! Yes! Quite so! Tell them, my good Abercorn, with my compliments, that we propose to rely on the sublime instincts of an ancient people!

⊰ MAIDEN SPEECHES ⊱

Into the euphoria of first being elected to the House of Commons – the congratulations of family, friends and new constituents, the thrill of seeing envelopes with 'MP' after one's name – gradually intrudes a profound question: when to make the maiden speech?

There are usually two approaches to this life choice: crack on and get it over with; or wait until most of the newcomers at a general election have done it and learn from their mistakes (the MP who comes in at a by-election has a lonelier vigil). And the MP who is returning to the House after losing at a previous election has no need to think of a maiden speech – you cannot regain your virginity.

The advice given to the new MP is: say something nice about your predecessor; something about your constituency; something about your aspirations – but don't make it too contentious or party political. Oh, and be witty and keep it to 10 minutes or so.

A maiden speech is by tradition not interrupted and heard in a silence broken only by laughter at the maiden's ready wit. Times change – Disraeli's maiden speech in December 1837 was howled down by the House (Disraeli wore *a bottle green frock coat, a white waistcoat laced with chains, and large fancy pantaloons*). Made to sit down, he shouted prophetically: *Though I sit down now, the time will come when you **shall** hear me.* This was something of poetic justice for Disraeli, who had recently described another maiden effort thus:

> *Mr Gibson Craig rose, stared like a stuck pig and said nothing. His friends cheered; he stammered; all cheered; then there was a dead and awful pause, and he sat down, and that was his performance.*

Disraeli was never short of confidence; in a letter to a friend four years before he entered the House of Commons, he said:

> *Between ourselves, I could floor them all. This entre nous: I was never more confident of anything than that I could carry everything before me in that House. The time will come.*

William Cobbett took a chance with his first speech in the Commons. He made it on his first night in the House, after the big names had spoken earlier in the debate, and began:

> *Mr Speaker, it appears to me that since I have been sitting here I have heard a great deal of vain and unprofitable conversation!*

In his maiden speech in 1906 F.E. Smith took a similar risk with an extraordinary denunciation of his political opponents in a *tour de force* that made his parliamentary reputation unassailable.

It is the custom for a maiden speaker to be congratulated by those who follow in the debate. When Herbert Morrison also turned his maiden speech into an attack on his political opponents, the Member who was called immediately afterwards began austerely:

> *It is the custom of this House to congratulate a maiden speaker. Sir, I do so.*

Churchill said of a hectoring maiden speech from a self-important new MP:

> *Call that a maiden speech? I call it a brazen hussy of a speech.*

An elegant example of the more usual congratulations to a maiden speaker comes from A.P. Herbert in November 1937:

> *I am quite sure that the noble Lady who has just delightfully delivered herself of her maiden speech will not misunderstand me if I say that I am sure that she feels, appropriately, as if she had just had a baby. I know that I did. As one who on that occasion did everything that was wrong and disgraced myself in every possible way, I most heartily offer the noble Lady congratulations, which I know will be shared by the entire House, on the modest, charming and witty way*

in which – not for the last time, I hope – she has spoken.

Herbert's reference to 'appropriately' was because the House was debating the second reading of the Population Bill.

⚔ PHINEAS FINN'S MAIDEN SPEECH ⚔

At last the member for East Barset sat down . . . and Phineas heard the president of that august assembly call upon himself to address the House. The thing was done. There he was with the House of Commons at his feet – a crowded House, bound to be his auditors as long as he should think fit to address them, and reporters by tens and twenties in the gallery ready and eager to let the country know what the young member for Loughshane would say in this his maiden speech . . .

He was cheered almost from the outset, and yet he knew as he went on that he was failing. He had certain arguments at his fingers' ends – points with which he was, in truth, so familiar that he need hardly have troubled himself to arrange them for special use – and he forgot even these. He found that he was going on with one platitude after another as to the benefit of reform, in a manner that would have shamed him six or seven years ago at a debating club. He pressed on, fearing that words would fail him altogether if he paused; but he did in truth speak very much too fast, knocking his words together so that no reporter could properly catch them. But he had nothing to say for the bill except what hundreds had said before, and hundreds would say again. . . . again he was cheered, by all around him – cheered as a new member is generally cheered – and in the midst of the cheer would have blown out his brains if there had been a pistol there ready for such an operation.

Anthony Trollope, *Phineas Finn* (1869)

⊰ SELECTION ⊱

Some time before the aspiring MP gets anywhere near a maiden speech, she or he must secure nomination as a PPC (prospective Parliamentary candidate). When Duff Cooper was given the once-over by the Conservatives of Stroud in 1924 he expected to be asked about Bills before Parliament (about which he knew little), and agriculture (about which he knew less). Neither subject arose. The selection committee wanted to know his religion, principally for the purpose of establishing that he was not a Roman Catholic; as Cooper said: *for the majority of English people, there are only two religions: Roman Catholic, which is wrong, and the rest, which don't matter*. The committee also wanted to know how much he would be able to contribute to the local Conservative Association. His expectations of being the next MP for Stroud were dashed when two days later he learned that *an older, possibly wiser and certainly much richer candidate had been selected.*

One of the more unusual exchanges at a selection interview took place when Michael Mates was being interviewed by the Conservative Association for the Petersfield constituency. The last question was: *Well, Colonel Mates, how long have you been a member of the Conservative Party?* A slightly nonplussed Mates had to say: *Er . . . I'm not actually a member. But if you select me I promise I'll join!*

Mates was selected, elected, and has been MP for Petersfield (later renamed East Hampshire) ever since.

⊰ HILAIRE BELLOC ⊱

Belloc was born near Paris in 1870, and educated at the Oratory School, Birmingham, and Balliol College, Oxford, where he became President of the Union. English by adoption, he nevertheless returned to France to do his military service in the artillery. His literary and journalistic output was astonishing (A.P. Herbert called him *the man who wrote a library*), amounting to 150 volumes.

In 1905 he stood as a Liberal in South Salford. The odds were against him. Not only had the constituency never returned a Liberal, but his deep attachment to Roman Catholicism was at odds with the solid non-conformism of his constituents. His agent advised him on no account to mention his Catholicism. This was a mistake. At his first public meeting as a candidate, Belloc began:

I am a Roman Catholic. This is my rosary. I tell it every day. I try to attend Mass every day. And if on account of my religion you decide not to elect me, then I shall daily thank God that He has spared me the indignity of being your representative.

Belloc arrived very late at another election meeting. Called upon to speak, he fixed the audience with a gaze and said:

I am late. It is entirely my fault. I do not apologise.

(In similar circumstances Churchill was asked why he was late and replied, unchallengeably: *Because I started late.*)

Belloc's non-conformist constituents elected him for South Salford in 1905; moreover, when he stood at the next election as an independent (having become disillusioned with the party system), they elected him again. In 1908 Belloc, long before his time, began to demand that the funds of political parties should be open to public audit.

E.C. Bentley, who invented the form of verse known as the Clerihew (from his middle name), said of Belloc:

Mr Hilaire Belloc
Is a case for legislation adhoc
He seems to think nobody minds
His books being all of different kinds

⊰ THE SPEAKER SEEKING RE-ELECTION ⊱

The Speaker seeking re-election is how the Speaker of the House of Commons is described at a general election and on the ballot paper. Having renounced party politics on being elected Speaker, he or she cannot fight an election under a party banner. Although upon a dissolution of Parliament the Speaker, like every other Member of the House, ceases to be an MP, he or she continues in the office of Speaker until re-elected or replaced in the new Parliament. So any canvassing is done as 'The Speaker seeking re-election'.

Bernard ('Jack') Weatherill (1920–2007), the much-loved Speaker of the House from 1983 to 1992, used to tell how he was canvassing in his Croydon North-West constituency, and towards the end of a long day reached the top of a tower block. He rang the bell, and after a while the letterbox flap opened. He knelt down, looked through, and found himself eye to eye with an evidently junior constituent.

Are your mother and father at home? asked Weatherill.

Me mum is. Who are you.?

Could you tell her, please, that it is The Speaker Seeking Re-Election?, said The Right Honourable Bernard Weatherill. The letterbox flap snaps shut, and small footsteps are heard running away into the distance. After a while they return. The letterbox flap opens again.

Did you ask her? asks the Speaker.

Yes.

And what did she say?

Me mum says, 'Sod off. Bloody gypsies.'

Mr Speaker Weatherill, by Robin-Lee Hall, 1991

Weatherill was apprenticed to the family tailoring business before becoming a cavalry officer in the Indian Army, and always had in his pocket a silver thimble – as he used to say, to remind him of his humbler past. When he first came into the House of Commons in 1964 he heard one knight of the shires say to another: *Good God, what is this place comin' to? D'ye know, I've just seen me tailor!*

He was also a highly competent Whip – most of the time. In the early days of a new Parliament, he sidled up to a new Member and said: *I've been reading all about you. You're exactly the sort of person we need on the Council of Europe delegation.* The new Member was overjoyed that his talents had been recognised so early in his career – until Weatherill came back a few minutes later. *I'm frightfully sorry. Could you remind me of your name?*

In Weatherill's early days in the Chair, the Labour MP Eric Heffer, goaded beyond endurance from the Conservative benches, snapped: *Shut up, you stupid git.* Weatherill intervened, saying mildly: *Order. I think I'm the one who's supposed to say that.*

Weatherill was the last Speaker to wear the full-bottomed wig, and the first to be televised in the Chair.

⚔ THE LARGEST CONSTITUENCY ⚔

The largest constituency is the Isle of Wight (electorate in 2005, 109,046). The smallest is Na h-Eileanan an Iar (formerly Western Isles), with an electorate in 2005 of 21,576.

⚔ UNSUCCESSFUL CANVASSING ⚔

Victor Meldrew, from the TV series *One Foot in the Grave*: *Vote for you? I'd rather stick my genitals in a pan of boiling chip fat.*

Told of **John Wilkes** (and of many others, including Nancy Astor and Winston Churchill):

Heckler: *Vote for you? I'd rather vote for the Devil.*
Candidate: *But in case your friend is not standing, may I count on your support?*

⊰ A DISSOLUTION OF PARLIAMENT, ⊱
VICTORIAN STYLE

These days we are used to the 24-hour news agenda, hundreds of commentators and pundits reading the runes, speculation about who might have booked advertising space, and so on. Few general elections come as a surprise. Things were a little different in the 1880s.

On 8 March 1880, **Disraeli** (by then the Earl of Beaconsfield) wrote to the Duke of Marlborough to say that he intended to seek a dissolution of Parliament and *afford an opportunity to the nation to decide upon a course which will materially influence its future fortunes and shape its destiny*.

Nothing was known of this letter (Dukes clearly did not leak) when Sir Stafford Northcote rose to make a statement in the Commons. Justin McCarthy, a Member at the time, described how Sir Stafford . . .

. . . spoke of the grave inconvenience that would be experienced by the Members of the House if they went into the country for Easter without knowing the intentions of the Government with respect to the Dissolution of Parliament. The moment that the Leader

of the House of Commons mentioned the word dissolution there was a literal flight of Members from the Chamber. Every man knew that the stroke had fallen, and every man was eager to send at once to his constituents the first news of the intended appeal to the country. In a few minutes the tidings were borne by a thousand wires to every electorate in the kingdom. It was computed, for the benefit of those who love the small statistics of great events, that some seven hundred and twenty telegrams were wired from the House of Commons on that night.

Disraeli's Conservative Party was heavily defeated in the general election that followed.

⚔ THE BY-ELECTION AT THE ANCIENT, ⚔ LOYAL AND PATRIOTIC BOROUGH OF EATANSWILL

From **Charles Dickens's** *Pickwick Papers* (1836–1837):
It was late in the evening when Mr Pickwick and his companions, assisted by Sam, dismounted from the roof of the Eatanswill coach. Large blue silk flags were flying from the windows of the Town Arms Inn, and bills were posted in every sash, intimating, in gigantic letters, that the Honourable Samuel Slumkey's committee sat there daily. A crowd of idlers were assembled in the road,

looking at a hoarse man in the balcony, who was apparently talking himself very red in the face in Mr Slumkey's behalf; but the force and point of whose arguments were somewhat impaired by the perpetual beating of four large drums which Mr Fizkin's committee had stationed at the street corner. There was a busy little man beside him, though, who took off his hat at intervals and motioned to the people to cheer, which they regularly did, most enthusiastically; and as the red-faced gentleman went on talking till he was redder in the face than ever, it seemed to answer his purpose quite as well as if anybody had heard him.

The Pickwickians had no sooner dismounted than they were surrounded by a branch mob of the honest and independent, who forthwith set up three deafening cheers, which being responded to by the main body (for it's not at all necessary for a crowd to know what they are cheering about), swelled into a tremendous roar of triumph, which stopped even the red-faced man in the balcony.

'Hurrah!' shouted the mob, in conclusion.

'One cheer more,' screamed the little fugleman in the balcony, and out shouted the mob again, as if lungs were cast-iron, with steel works.

'Slumkey for ever!' roared the honest and independent.

'Slumkey for ever!' echoed Mr Pickwick, taking off his hat.

'No Fizkin!' roared the crowd.

'Certainly not! shouted Mr Pickwick.

'*Hurrah!*' *And then there was another roaring, like that of a whole menagerie when the elephant has rung the bell for the cold meat.*

'*Who is Slumkey?*' *whispered Mr Tupman.*

'*I don't know,*' *replied Mr Pickwick in the same tone.* '*Hush. Don't ask any questions. It's always best on these occasions to do what the mob do.*'

But suppose there are two mobs?' *suggested Mr Snodgrass.*

'*Shout with the largest,*' *replied Mr Pickwick.*

Election Sketches: the 1880 General Election, the Illustrated London News, *1880*

⊰ THE GENERAL LOSES IT ⊱

An occasion to be cherished in that election of 1880 was the speech of **Major-General Feilden** to an appreciative audience in North Lancashire. The event was notable for three things: first, that the reporter from the *Preston Guardian* was able to make such a complete record; second, that his newspaper printed it; and third, that the good General was able to keep upright, because he was clearly in the state sometimes known as 'hog-whimpering'. What follows is only a small fragment:

> *Major-General Feilden, who on rising was received with loud cheers, said: Ladies and gentlemen, electors of North Lancashire, the first words I say to you are these: I love Blackpool; I lived here during the whole years of my boy-hood, as a school-boy. I come here every year of my life. I hope before long to take a house here, and bring my children among you. Yes, I do; I do. Now, mind, I don't say this by way of flattering you. I don't indeed. I wouldn't go to Parliament under any such circumstances. No, I wouldn't. If you don't think I'm worthy of going to Parliament, I won't go. I don't want to go. If you think I have any qualities which are likely to fit me to be a fit Member of Parliament, then send me. If not, don't; no, don't. I say no, don't. Send Mr Storey . . .*
>
> *Gentlemen, it has never — I say it has never been my ambition. I wish to do what is my duty. I am nobody myself, but my friends say I must go. I have been advised to come. I mean, I have been advised to come forward by*

men whose opinions I value. I met a particular friend of mine in Preston the other day, and I said to him, 'Now, look here', says I, 'do you think a change of government would do?' I said, distinctly, 'Do you think a change in Parliament would benefit the country?' He said, 'No, I dont.' He said emphatically, 'No, I don't.' I don't believe it would.' And so I said, I said . . . 'Neither do I.' And I don't.

I have been advised to come forward by men whom I love, and I've come, and I'm here before you tonight. If you think, after hearing what I have to say, I shall be any use to you, send me. And if you don't . . . don't send me. I have been a soldier all my life . . . My father used to come here. If I live a little longer I shall have property here. I don't say this as an inducement for you to vote for me, but I hope you will. I have been a soldier all my life. Honestly I come before you tonight. Colonel Stanley has been with me at Kirkham. Mr Cocker and gentlemen, he would have come here tonight only he couldn't. I mean he would have been in this room with me tonight if he could have done so . . . I am very sorry he is not here tonight to see this glorious room. I have never in my lifetime, I couldn't have conceived that I should have been in such a position as I find myself tonight on this platform. Truly and honestly I couldn't have thought it. I don't wish too much enthusiasm.

A Voice: 'Sit thi sel' down; tha's said enough.'

I'll sit down if you think I've said enough. [Shouts of 'Go on'.] In cases of elections it is said you must go just a little to extremes . . . there are circumstances under which you may be carried for a little moment into enthusiasm, and I conceive this to be one of those cases. [Cheers.]

I cannot suppose that anything I can say will be much to my advantage. [Pause of half a minute, and cries of 'Go on'.] I am going on as fast as I can . . . I say this as a simple man . . . As a matter of fact, I assure you that I am a soldier in the British Army and a Major General. I have no occupation. I have nothing to do . . . And therefore I think I am right, and I propose myself as your Member to back up the throne, to back up the throne, to back up the throne, gentlemen, and help the religion of the country . . .

I am a simple man. All I can say – if you return me to Parliament; if you think I am worth anything at all, I will support the cause of England, and religion, and Queen Victoria [Laughter.] . . . If the opposition party come into power we do not know what will happen. [Hear, hear.] I must say this change of Government is a great and grievous mistake. You remember the old trite – trite – trite – trite I say trite remark of, let me see . . . Abraham Lincoln. 'Don't swop horses in crossing streams.' [Laughter.]

It is the only country in the world, Mr Chairman. We have colonies in every direction. Lord Beaconsfield's Government has done everything which is heroic. [Cheers.] . . . I come now because I think it is my duty to help in the present crisis of the history of England. [Applause.] . . . If you think I am wrong, don't send me to Parliament.

If you think I am right, do. If you don't think proper to support me, don't do so. [Hear, hear, and applause.]

Major-General Feilden was elected.

⊰ COAL FOR VOTES ⊱

From the diary of the **Rev. Francis Kilvert** (Monday, 22 February 1875):

John Knight of the Copse in our parish [Langley Burrell in Wiltshire] . . . was very much discontented and indignant because none of Mr Goldney MP's gifts of coal etc. had come to him. 'I shall never vote for Mr Goldney again,' he said. I suggested that people were not supposed to sell their votes, but to vote according to their conscience. 'I do so,' he said, 'but I shall never vote for Mr Goldney again.'

He felt the more aggrieved because some coal or money had gone to the Bremhill people who were not in the borough and had no vote. The agent who distributed the MP's gifts told John Knight there was not enough to go round. 'Of course there isn't,' said John, 'if you give it away to people who have no vote.' So much for electioneering, and the efficacy of the bribery bill. It is all corruption, corruption, corruption.

⚔ **RESIGNATION** ⚔

An MP cannot resign his or her seat, but must apply to be appointed to *an office of profit under the Crown*, thus joining the civil servants, members of the armed forces, judges, police, and a host of paid members of public bodies listed in Schedule 1 to the House of Commons Disqualification Act 1975. The origins of this lie in the 17th century; in 1624 the House resolved that *a man, after he is chosen, cannot relinquish*; and in 1680, no doubt on the basis that receiving money from a Crown appointment would be a conflict of loyalties, the House resolved:

> *That no Member of this House shall accept of any Office, or Place of Profit, from the Crown, without the leave of this House, or any Promise of any such Office, or Place of Profit, during such time as he shall continue a Member of this House.*

> *That all offenders herein shall be expelled this House.*

The offices of profit used to provide the necessary disqualification for an MP who wishes to leave the House are: steward or bailiff of Her Majesty's three Chiltern Hundreds of Stoke, Desborough and Burnham (thus the phrase 'taking the Chiltern Hundreds') or that of the steward of the Manor of Northstead. (Other offices formerly used for the same purpose, but no longer, were the Manors of Old Shoreham, East Hendred, Poynings and Hempholme, and the Escheatorships of Munster and Ulster.)

The **Hundred of Stoke** has 14 parishes including Stoke Poges, Eton and Slough; the **Hundred of Desborough** contains 17 parishes, including Great Marlow, Stokenchurch and High Wycombe; and the **Hundred of Burnham** has 13 parishes including Beaconsfield, Chalfont St Giles and Farnham Royal. Although real enough in the past, these offices are nowadays legal fictions: the inhabitants of those parts of Buckingham and Berkshire would be a little surprised to find a departing MP doing any stewarding or bailiffing.

The offices are in the gift of the Chancellor of the Exchequer, and the Treasury writes a formal letter of appointment to the Member concerned, who holds the office until he or she applies to be released, or until another Member wishes to resign.

The most recent appointments have been: Chiltern Hundreds: Tony Blair (June 2007) when he resigned as Prime Minister; David Davis (June 2008) Shadow Home Secretary, who resigned to fight a by-election in his constituency to draw attention to his criticisms of Government policy; and Ian Gibson (June 2009); and Northstead: Boris Johnson, Member for Henley (June 2008) following his election as Mayor of London; David Marshall (June 2008) because of ill-health; and Michael Martin (June 2009).

During the Second World War the rule preventing Members of Parliament from holding offices of profit under the Crown was suspended by the House of Commons (Temporary

Provisions) Acts which were passed in each year from 1941 to 1944 and by the House of Commons (Service in His Majesty's Forces) Act 1939. In 1941 some 200 MPs (including Ministers) were involved in Government service and a further 116 were serving in the armed forces.

In the Lords, a Member who does not wish to attend may apply for leave of absence, but may not resign. And unlike the Commons, the Lords may not expel one of its Members; legislation is required. In 1919 the Dukes of Albany and Cumberland, two peers who also happened to be German princes and who had supported the King's enemies during the First World War were, under the Titles Deprivation Act 1919, stripped of their privileges as peers.

⊰ THERE HAVE BEEN 17 ⊱ GENERAL ELECTIONS

There have been 17 general elections since the Second World War. Two took place in February (1950 and 1974), one in March (1966), one in April (1992), four in May (1955, 1979, 1997 and 2005), four in June (1970, 1983, 1987 and 2001), one in July (1945) and four in October (1951, 1959, 1964, 1974).

The last general election not on a **Thursday** was on Tuesday 27 October 1931.

The habit of holding general elections on Thursdays is said to be the result of lobbying by weekly country newspapers who published on Saturdays. A Thursday was the latest day on which the Saturday paper could carry the results.

◄ THE SECRET BALLOT ►

The secret ballot at parliamentary elections was introduced in 1872 as a temporary measure subject to annual review. It was established as a permanent rule in 1918.

◄ THE 1945 GENERAL ELECTION ►

From **Sir Winston Churchill's** *The Gathering Storm* (1948):
On the night of the tenth of May [1940], at the outset of this mighty battle, I acquired the chief power in the State, which henceforth I wielded in ever-growing measure for five years and three months of world war, at the end of which time, all our enemies having surrendered unconditionally or being about to do so, I was immediately dismissed by the British electorate from all further conduct of their affairs.

IX
'WOMEN'S PASSIONS ARE INFINITELY MORE VIOLENT'

*It is necessary to remind the House that women's
passions are infinitely more violent when
called forth than men's.*
Earl Percy, speaking in the House of Lords
against votes for women (1873)

⊰ VOTES FOR WOMEN ⊱

Mary Wollstonecraft is usually regarded as the first campaigner for **female equality**; her *A Vindication of the Rights of Woman* was published in 1792. The first debate in the Commons was on 20 May 1867 and was initiated by John Stuart Mill. Thereafter there were attempts to legislate in most sessions for the next 50 years. The thoughts of opponents give some idea of the difficulties to be overcome:

The character of the legislation of a woman-chosen Parliament will be the increased importance which would be given to questions of a quasi-social or philanthropic character, viewed with regard to the supported interests or the partisan bias of special classes rather than to the broader considerations of the public weal. We shall have more wars for an idea or hasty alliances with scheming neighbours, more class cries, permissive legislation, domestic perplexities and sentimental grievances. Our legislation will develop hysterical and spasmodic features, partaking more of the French and American system rather than reproducing the character of the English Parliament.

Alexander Beresford Hope (1871)

The banner unfurled from the Ladies' Gallery in the House of Commons during a protest in 1908

The idea of trying out this dangerous idea somewhere else evidently appealed:

This is an experiment so large and bold that it ought to be tried by some other country first.

James Bryce (1892)

The possible characteristics of women MPs were used as arguments against votes for women:

Intellectually women have not got the gifts which fit them for being elected. They have got a certain amount of what I might call instinct rather than reason . . . they are impulsive, emotional and have got absolutely no sense of proportion.

Henry Labouchère (1897)

Labouchère was at least consistent. Eight years later, he told the House:

Women have at present such an influence over the actions of men that if they had been really united in the desire for the franchise they would have got it long ago. It is only a few women with masculine minds who take an interest in politics and desire to have votes.

Sir Frederick Banbury (1905):

I am sure that we would never be able to convince a woman in this House if she did not wish to be convinced. I believe that there are very few instances of any Member having changed his vote by anything said in debate, but I am quite certain that if women are introduced into this House it would be useless to debate any point at all because the women will have made up their minds before the debate begins.

Austen Chamberlain (1913):

For political functions it is not a question of the equality of men or women but it is the question of the suitability of the peculiar quality of the two sexes for the exercise of special and particular functions and, in my opinion, if I can put it without unnecessary offence, the qualities of women . . . are not qualities by which we desire to be governed . . . In my opinion, mentally, physiologically and physically there is a real differentiation in these matters between men and women which the law does not create, the law cannot remedy and which we have got to reckon with.

The best known campaign for **votes for women** was the Women's Social and Political Union, founded in 1903 by Emmeline Pankhurst.

Emmeline Pankhurst (1858–1928)

In 1916 it became clear that the **electoral registers were hopelessly out of date** because of the movement of military personnel. Millicent Garrett Fawcett persuaded the Prime Minister, Asquith, that the issue should be formally considered and a Speaker's Conference on Electoral Reform was set up, and recommended (limited) votes for women.

On 6 February 1918 Royal Assent was given to the **Representation of the People Act 1918**. Section 4 read:

> 4. – (1) A woman shall be entitled to be registered as a parliamentary elector for a constituency if she –
>> (a) has attained the age of thirty years;
>> (b) is not subject to any legal incapacity; and
>> (c) is entitled to be registered as a local government elector in respect of the occupation in that constituency of land or premises (not being a dwelling-house) of a yearly value of not less than five pounds or of a dwelling-house, or is the wife of a husband entitled to be so registered.

Votes for women of over 30 (with a property qualification) was rather strange as later that year it became lawful for a woman to stand for Parliament at 21, nine years younger than she could vote for anyone else.

In 1928 the Representation of the People (Equal Franchise) Act **reduced the voting age to 21**, the same as for men. In 1969 the voting age was reduced to 18 for both men and women.

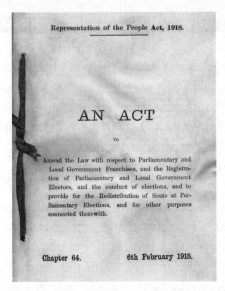

Representation of the People Act, 1918.

AN ACT

TO

Amend the Law with respect to Parliamentary and Local Government Franchises, and the Registration of Parliamentary and Local Government Electors, and the conduct of elections, and to provide for the Redistribution of Seats at Parliamentary Elections, and for other purposes connected therewith.

Chapter 64.   6th February 1918.

The record copy of the Representation of the People Act, 1918

❧ PARLIAMENT ❧ (QUALIFICATION OF WOMEN) ACT 1918

Acts do not have to be lengthy in order to make historic changes:
    1. Capacity of women to be members of Parliament
A woman shall not be disqualified by sex or marriage for being elected to or sitting or voting as a Member of the Commons House of Parliament.
    2. Short title
This Act may be cited as the Parliament (Qualification of Women) Act 1918.

Royal Assent, 21 November 1918

❧ WOMEN IN THE HOUSE OF COMMONS ❧

At the 1918 general election which followed the passing of that Act, only 17 out of 1,623 candidates were women. Christabel Pankhurst (daughter of Emmeline Pankhurst, founder of the Women's Social and Political Union) polled more votes than any of the other women candidates but was defeated by 775 votes.

The only successful candidate had been rather limited in her campaign as she spent it in a cell in Holloway Prison. Countess Markievicz was being held under suspicion of having supported Germany during the war (for which there appears to have been no evidence). She won the St Patrick's division of Dublin but, as a protest against the British Government's policy on Ireland, never took her seat.

The first woman to sit in the House of Commons was Nancy Astor (Viscountess Astor) who was elected for Plymouth Sutton in 1919 when her husband, the sitting Member, succeeded to his father's peerage. The next two women MPs also took over their husband's seats: Margaret Wintringham (Liberal) for Louth in 1921 (her husband had died; she did not speak in public during the campaign as a mark of respect); and Mabel Phillipson (Conservative) for Berwick-upon-Tweed in 1923 after her husband had lost his seat because of fraud by his election agent.

The first female Labour MP to be elected was Arabella Lawrence (East Ham North) in 1923.

Margaret Thatcher, interview with the *Liverpool Post* (1974):
It will be years before a woman either leads the Party or becomes Prime Minister. I certainly do not expect to see it happening in my lifetime.

The post of Chancellor of the Exchequer is the only one of the four great offices of state (Prime Minister, Foreign Secretary, Home Secretary, Chancellor) not yet to have been held by a woman.

⊰ THE FIRST WOMEN ⊱

The first female Minister was Margaret Bondfield, elected in 1923, who in January 1924 became Under Secretary in the Minister of Labour in Ramsay MacDonald's Government. In 1929 (after losing her seat and returning at a by-election) she became the first woman Cabinet Minister as Minister of Labour, and the first female politician Privy Counsellor.

The first female Prime Minister was Margaret Thatcher following the 1979 general election, which also returned the lowest number of women MPs (19) since the 17 at the 1951 election.

The first female Speaker was Betty Boothroyd, formerly a Deputy Speaker, who was elected Speaker on 27 April 1992 and served until 2000.

The first woman to sit in the Speaker's Chair was Betty Harvie Anderson, who became a Deputy Speaker in July 1970.

⊰ PERCENTAGES ⊱

Before the Second World War, the **highest percentage of female MPs** was following the 1931 election, at 2.4% (15 MPs). Between 1945 and 1983 the proportion was between 2.7% and 4.6%. In 1987 it was 6.3% (41) and in 1992 9.2% (60).

The number of female MPs doubled to 120 (18.2% of the House) in 1997, and rose to 128 (19.8%) in the 2005 election. During the 2005 Parliament, the deaths of Patsy Calton, Rachel Squire and Gwyneth Dunwoody (and the return of male MPs at the by-elections) reduced the number to 125 (19.3%).

The 2001 Census showed that women made up **51.4% of the population** of the United Kingdom.

⚜ WOMEN IN PARLIAMENT: ⚜
THE INTERNATIONAL LEAGUE

The Inter-Parliamentary Union in Geneva compiles comparative figures for the lower Houses of Parliaments around the world. The **highest proportion of women** (56.3%) is in the Rwandan Parliament.

The others in the top 10 are Sweden, Cuba, Finland, the Netherlands, Argentina, Denmark, Angola, Costa Rica and Spain, with percentages ranging from 47% down to 36.3%.

The **UK** is 60th with 19.3%, below countries such as Afghanistan, Lesotho, Pakistan and Ethiopia.

France comes 66th (18.2%) and the **United States** 71st (17%).

⚜ WOMEN IN THE HOUSE OF LORDS ⚜

In 1855 **Lord Redesdale complained** that the presence of so many women to hear an important debate had created a frivolous atmosphere and had even discouraged a colleague from addressing the House:

The habit of surrounding a house of debate with that which was, no doubt, most beautiful, but which here was out of place, made your Lordships' House look more like a casino than anything else.

Lords Hansard (18 May 1855)

Just over a hundred years later, in debate on the Life Peerages Bill, the **Earl of Glasgow** told the Lords:

Women . . . are not suited to politics, for the following reasons. They are often moved by their hearts more than they are by their heads, and the emotional urge which exists in a woman's make-up does not help towards good judgement . . . Many of us do not want women in this House. We do not want to sit beside them on the Benches, nor do we want to meet them in the Library. This is a House of men, a House of Lords. We do not wish it to become a House of Lords and Ladies.

Lords Hansard (31 October 1957)

The Life Peerages Bill received Royal Assent on 30 April 1958, and on 24 July the first 14 life peers were announced. Four were women: Baroness Swanborough, Baroness Ravensdale, Baroness Wootton of Abinger and Baroness Elliot of Harwood.

In 2009 there were **147 women** in the House of Lords, 19.7% of the total, and almost exactly the same proportion as in the House of Commons.

❧ MORE ENLIGHTENMENT ❧

On the **education of children**:

> *It has been said that children should be kept at school until 14 years of age; but the amount and importance of the labour which lads between 10 and 14 can perform should not be ignored. Since the present educational system has come into operation, the weeds have very much multiplied in Norfolk which was once regarded as quite the garden of England, weeding being peculiarly the work of children whose labour is cheap, whose sight is keen, bodies flexible and fingers nimble.*

Earl Fortescue (1880)

On **votes for all**:

> *If this principle of individual suffrage be granted and be carried to its utmost extent, it goes to subvert the peerage, to depose the King, and to extinguish every hereditary distinction and privileged order and to establish that system of equalising anarchy announced in the French legislation and attested in the blood of the massacres at Paris. The question then is whether you will abide by your constitution or hazard a change with all that dreadful train of consequences.*

William Pitt the Younger (1793)

> *. . . it is the wildest fancy that could possibly enter into the conception of any human being.*

Lord Holland (1817)

How can security for any consistent line of policy in the government be obtained when in the event of a Dissolution of Parliament each Minister must depend on the caprice of popular opinion . . . for his return to Parliament?

4th Marquess of Salisbury (father of the Prime Minister) (1832)

On **slavery**:

The Africans are accustomed to slavery in their own country and the taking of them to another quarter of the globe is therefore no great hardship.

Sir William Young (1804)

Nothing good can be expected from it. I would venture to say that it is to the existence of the slave trade that your Lordships are indebted for their being now sitting in this place. Our existence depends on the strength of our navy and the strength of our navy is chiefly derived from the slave trade.

The Earl of Westmoreland (1807) speaking on the last day of the last debate on Lord Grenville's Bill to make slavery unlawful.

When the Bill was passed, Grenville said:

I congratulate the House on having now performed one of the most glorious acts that have ever been done by any assembly of any nation in the world.

⋇ *ENTENTE CORDIALE* ⋇

When the Lords debated slavery in 1793, the **Earl of Abingdon** argued that the abolitionists were furthering the pernicious principles of the French Revolution:

> . . . *that new philosophy containing, like Pandora's box, all the evils and vices that human nature or the world can be afflicted with . . . the principles held by those monsters in human shape, I mean the people of France, a race of people descended from monkeys and from wolves; for when they are not skipping and dancing like monkeys, they are ravenous and ferocious as wolves. If the French principles prevail, we shall sink into the same abyss of misery with them, and be what they are . . . better were it for us that we were created toads, to live on the fumes of a dunghill.*

His Lordship then moved:

> *That the further consideration of the Question for the abolition of the slave trade be postponed to this day five months.*

X
QUESTION !

*To ask the Prime Minister, if he will list his
engagements...*
(format of most Questions to the Prime Minister)

The first Parliamentary Question was asked in 1721, in the
House of Lords.

Arthur Balfour, Prime Minister 1902–1905, had **an intense
dislike of Parliamentary Questions**, describing them as:
*piles of rubbish with which, for purposes of self-advertise-
ment, Members now crowd the Order Paper.*

The Table Office of the House of Commons deals with
an average of 619 Parliamentary Questions (PQs) every
sitting day. In session 2008–2009, **75,601 answers** to
written PQs were published. The 20 MPs who tabled the
most PQs accounted for a quarter of the total, an average
of nearly a thousand each.

⊸ HOW DO PMQs WORK? ⊱

PMQs, or Prime Minister's Questions, take place every Wednesday when the House of Commons is sitting, from 12 noon to 12.30pm. They are the highest-profile part of the sitting week, televised live and the Chamber packed with Members.

On the Order Paper will be the names of 15 MPs who wish to ask a question (almost always in the form 'If he will list his official engagements for . . . [that day]'). Because there are so many MPs competing, many parliamentary opportunities in the Commons are allocated by ballot, including the first 20 slots to introduce a Private Member's Bill, the chance to have one of the half-hour 'Adjournment Debates' on four days of the week (the fifth is chosen by the Speaker), and the chance to ask oral Questions of Ministers.

The most hotly contested of these ballots is that for Prime Minister's Questions. 300 to 400 MPs will put their names in to the Table Office three sitting days beforehand. Their names are selected at random by computer, and the top 15 names appear on the Order Paper, thus:

The Speaker calls the first MP, who says simply: *Number One, Sir.* The answer the Prime Minister gives is just as formulaic as the first Question printed on the Order Paper: *This morning I had meetings with Ministerial colleagues and others. In addition to my duties in this House, I shall have further such meetings later today.*

No. 111   2783

House of Commons

Wednesday 15 July 2009

Order of Business

At 12 noon

Oral Questions to the Prime Minister

Unless otherwise indicated the Members listed below will ask a Question without notice.

* Q1 **Mr John Maples** (Stratford-on-Avon): If he will list his official engagements for Wednesday 15 July. (286657)

* Q2 **Charles Hendry** (Wealden): (286658)

* Q3 **Alistair Burt** (North East Bedfordshire): (286659)

* Q4 **Judy Mallaber** (Amber Valley): (286660)

* Q5 **Julie Morgan** (Cardiff North): (286661)

* Q6 **Mr Gregory Campbell** (East Londonderry): (286662)

* Q7 **Dr Julian Lewis** (New Forest East): Whether insuring against the threat of state-versus-state warfare remains a core role of the armed forces; and if he will make a statement. (286663)

* Q8 **Mr Richard Spring** (West Suffolk): (286664)

* Q9 **Mr Stephen O'Brien** (Eddisbury): (286665)

* Q10 **Paul Holmes** (Chesterfield): (286666)

* Q11 **Andrew Stunell** (Hazel Grove): (286667)

* Q12 **Mr Virendra Sharma** (Ealing Southall): (286668)

* Q13 **Andrew Gwynne** (Denton & Reddish): (286669)

* Q14 **Linda Gilroy** (Plymouth, Sutton): (286670)

* Q15 **Bill Wiggin** (Leominster): (286671)

Prime Minister's Questions: part of the House of Commons Order Paper

The Speaker then calls the first MP to ask a supplementary question. This can be about anything at all which is within the Prime Minister's responsibilities, and the PM gives his reply. (There is a natural temptation for MPs on his own side to ask the PM about the Opposition's policies, for which he is not responsible, and the Speaker will then intervene.)

The Speaker takes questioners from each side of the Chamber in turn, thus alternating Government and Opposition Members. Because the 15 MPs successful in the ballot are unlikely to be from alternate sides, the Speaker will need to call other MPs (who leap to their feet hoping to be noticed) to keep to the pattern. These other supplementaries are often called 'free hits'.

When it's the turn of the **Opposition side**, the Leader of the Opposition will be called as soon as he stands up (often near the beginning of PMQs). He gets six questions, which he can take as two lots of three or, more often, in a run of six in frequently heated exchanges with the PM. When he has finished his ration the Speaker will call someone from the Government side, and then the Leader of the Liberal Democrats, who gets two questions.

Because of **the profile of PMQs**, the staff at Number 10 put a great deal of effort into predicting things likely to come up and providing the necessary briefing. They may well suggest to a backbencher on the Government side a 'good news' topic that will allow the PM to have a ready-made 'good news' answer. He will not have notice of likely supplementaries from the Opposition except when an MP is successful in the ballot and wants to raise a non-partisan (especially constituency) matter. Then, instead of the PM saying that he will write, the MP gets a fuller answer which will give the constituency matter a higher profile (and, by the way, make the Prime Minister look omniscient).

PMQs can be rowdy, and the occasion has its critics, who see in it the worst of 'yah-boo' politics. But among the nations of the world it is also a rare example of the Head of Government being subjected to questioning every week in Parliament.

⊰ WHY IS THE PM ALWAYS ASKED ⊱ ABOUT HIS ENGAGEMENTS?

On the face of it, this seems a **strange** way to use the opportunity to ask the PM an oral Question in prime time. The habit arose more than 30 years ago. If an MP put on the Order Paper a question to the PM about defence or agriculture, say, it would be transferred to the Minister responsible, and the MP would have lost his balloted opportunity to ask an oral Question.

At the request of a backbencher, the Clerks in the Table Office devised a question not only that could not be transferred but also that could be repeated week after week (because under the rules of the House a Parliamentary Question which is fully answered cannot be asked again in the same session unless there are new circumstances). No-one but the PM is responsible for his own engagements, so he cannot transfer it; and the engagements differ from week to week, so the question can always be in order.

When Margaret Thatcher became Prime Minister, she let it be known that she would always answer questions on individual Ministers' responsibilities rather than transferring them (and indeed seemed to take some relish in doing so); and every PM since has taken the same line.

But the vast majority of MPs still go on putting down the 'engagements' question. It's always topical – just in case something hits the headlines after they have tabled their question three days before – and because there are odds of more than 20 to 1 of being successful in the ballot, there's not a lot of point in thinking up a specific question in advance. Today, the Order Paper recognises the reality; although Members have tabled the 'engagements' question, it is their intention to ask a 'question without notice' which appears on the Order Paper (see page 192).

⊰ TONY BLAIR'S LAST ANSWER ⊱

Tony Blair's last answer in PMQs was:

Mr Speaker, if I may finish with two brief remarks – first to the House. I have never pretended to be a great House of Commons man, but I pay the House the greatest compliment I can by saying that, from first to last, I never stopped fearing it. The tingling apprehension that I felt at three minutes to 12 today I felt as much 10 years ago. It is in that fear that respect is contained.

The second thing that I would like to say is about politics and to all my colleagues from different political parties. Some may belittle politics but we who are engaged in it know that is where people stand tall. Although I know that it has many harsh connotations, it is still the arena that sets the heart beating a little faster. If it is, on occasions, the place of low skulduggery, it is more often the place for the pursuit of noble causes. I wish everyone, friend or foe, well. That's that. The end.

⊰ PRECISE ANSWERS ⊱

From Hansard (3 February 1992):

Mr Skinner: *To ask the Minister for the Civil Service, how many Civil Servants in employment at the latest available date are (a) men and (b) women.*

Mr Renton: *All of them.*

(The phrasing of statistical questions can be a trap for the unwary: it is tempting to ask for the numbers of people 'broken down by sex and age' but rather harder to give an accurate answer as to their physical state.)

From Hansard (2 June 1980):

Dr Mawhinney: *To ask the Attorney-General, how many circulars and other forms of general guidance his Department issued during the months January to April in 1978, 1979 and 1980?*

The Attorney-General: *None, none, none.*

Stephen Leacock on Parliamentary Questions:

Looking around to find just where the natural service of the House of Commons comes in, I am inclined to think that it must be in the practice of 'asking Questions' in the House. Whenever anything goes wrong a Member rises and asks a Question. He gets up, for example, with a little paper in his hand, and asks the Government if Ministers are aware that the Khedive of Egypt was seen yesterday wearing a Turkish tarboosh. Ministers say very humbly that they hadn't known it, and a thrill runs through the whole country.

The Members can apparently ask any question they like. In the repeated visits which I made to the gallery of the House of Commons I was unable to find any particular sense or meaning in the questions asked, though no doubt they had an intimate bearing on English politics not clear to an outsider like myself. I heard one Member ask the Government whether they were aware that herrings were being imported from Hamburg to Harwich. The Government said no.

Another Member rose and asked the Government whether they considered Shakespeare or Molière to be the greater dramatic artist. The Government answered that Ministers were taking this under their earnest consideration and that a report would be submitted to Parliament.

Another Member asked the Government if they knew who had won the Queen's Plate this season at Toronto. They did; in fact, this Member got it wrong, as this is the very thing that the Government do know. Towards the close of the evening a Member rose and asked the Government if they knew what time it was. The Speaker, however, ruled this question out of order on the ground that it had been answered before.

My Discovery of England, 1922

◄ SOME MORE ANSWERS ►

First, a little worryingly . . . (from Hansard, 7 December 1979):

Mr Michael Brown: *To ask the Secretary of State for Industry, if he will make a statement on the future of the United Kingdom.*

Mr Michael Marshall: *I will reply to my honourable Friend as soon as possible.*

From Hansard (27 December 2006):

Mr Graham Brady: *To ask the Secretary of State for*

Foreign and Commonwealth Affairs, what responsibility the Minister for Europe has for Ugandan affairs.
Mr Hoon [holding answer 23 November 2006]: *I only have responsibility for Ugandan affairs where they relate specifically to European matters. These activities do not constitute a significant part of my ministerial workload.*

From Hansard (9 February 1983):

Mr Graham: *To ask the Secretary of State for Foreign and Commonwealth Affairs, why a payment of £341 was made by the Foreign and Commonwealth Office to Palestine for 1981–82, as listed in the Appropriation Accounts for that year.*

Mr Hurd: *When the mandate for Palestine terminated in 1948 certain liabilities of the former Palestine Government remained outstanding to be met by Her Majesty's Government.*

The payment of £341 listed under subhead 'B4: Palestine' in the 1981-82 Appropriation Accounts was for a new artificial leg for Mr M.A. Issa, who used to work for the former Palestine Government.

ORDER! ORDER!

⊰ AN ODD EXCHANGE ⊱

Every now and again one comes across Parliamentary
Questions that seem to have **a whole novel** in them . . .
From Hansard (1 July 1918):

MUSWELL HILL SHOOTING CASE

Major Newman *asked the Home Secretary whether the
condition of an uninterned enemy alien named
Wohlgemuth, of Church Crescent, Muswell Hill, N., who
was recently shot by his wife, is now such that he can give
some account of himself; whether such account shows that
he came to England in 1887, is a qualified doctor, and is
besides a sausage-skin manufacturer and an experimental
chemist carrying out Government work; and, having
regard to the evidence of his love of country given by his
wife, should he be still alive and recover is it intended to
allow him to continue his manufacturing and experimental
work in an internment camp and not in Muswell Hill?*

Mr. Hewins: *The person named is not an enemy alien. He
is a British subject, having been granted naturalisation in
1897. I am informed that he came to this country in 1887,
that he holds the honorary degree of Doctor of Science at
University College, that he is a partner in a firm of
sausage-skin dealers, and that he has had contracts with
the Admiralty for gold-beater's skin. Before he is
discharged from hospital full inquiry will be made as to the
foundation, if any, for the accusations of disloyalty to this
country made against him by his wife, who is charged with
shooting him, and any action that may be called for in the
public interest will be taken.*

◄ MORE OLD CHESTNUTS ►

A Minister and the Permanent Secretary of his Department were being driven to a distant engagement. The fog closed in, the car went more and more slowly, and it became clear to them that they were lost. Dimly through the fog they could see a figure shambling towards them. *Quick, ask him where we are*, said the Minister to the driver. *You're in Wales, in a car, in the fog*, said the figure, and shambled off into the gloom. Silence fell. After a while the Permanent Secretary said: *Do you know, Minister, that's the perfect answer to a Parliamentary Question. It's short, it's absolutely accurate, and it tells you nothing that you didn't know already.*

Of the prayers read by the Speaker's Chaplain at the start of each day's sitting . . . *The Chaplain looks at the Members and prays for the country.*

A Welsh MP, at a meeting in his constituency to adopt him as the candidate for the forthcoming general election, and seeking to impress with an account of his extraordinary hard work and assiduity: *In the last session, I have asked no fewer than* three hundred and eighty-seven *Parliamentary Questions.*
 Voice from the back: *Ignorant bugger.*

A sporting peer becomes convinced that his trainer is doping his horses and starts haunting the training stables expecting to find his worst suspicions confirmed, but to no effect. One day at the races one of his horses is running and, in a strong field, is a rank outsider. In the paddock the peer sees the trainer give something to the horse. He swoops: *What the hell is that?* The trainer thinks on his feet: *Just a sweet, my Lord. Assyrian Lancer has a very sweet tooth, as you know. Quite harmless, of course. Indeed, I think I'll have one myself. For you, my Lord?* And they both have one of the pastilles.

The trainer saddles the horse and gives the jockey his last-minute instructions: *Lie back about fourth or fifth. Keep Wallflower and Hopalong in your sights. Then when you come round the final turn with half a mile to go, give it everything you've got. The only things likely to pass you after that will be his Lordship or me.*

A new MP sitting on the green benches for the first time, to old stager next to him: *It's so exciting! At last, looking across at our enemies!* Old stager: *No, those are your opponents. Your enemies are on this side.*

Leo Abse (1917–2008), the colourful MP for Pontypool and social reformer, was being introduced at inordinate length at a meeting by a chairman who pronounced his name 'Abs' instead of 'Absy'. It was 'Mr Abs this' and 'Mr Abs' that. Finally Abse could stand it no longer: *Call me Absy*, he hissed at the Chairman. *Well, now, that's very kind of you*, the beaming chairman responded, *You can call me Jonesy.*

Abse used Private Member's Bills to bring about historic social change. After two of his Bills to reform the law on homosexuality had been blocked, he finally achieved his aim with the Sexual Offences Act 1967; and his Matrimonial Causes and Reconciliation Bill of 1962 led four years later to legislation allowing divorce on the irretrievable breakdown of marriage.

Of a debate: *Everything has been said . . . but not yet by everyone.*

Lord Grocott said in the House of Lords on 12 March 2007, announcing the arrangements for a heavily over-subscribed debate on Lords reform:

> *With some diffidence, I recommend to the House something that, to my knowledge, has never happened in either House of Parliament in the entirety of their histories – that it would greatly assist the speed of the debate if Members did not deploy arguments that had previously been made.*

Noble Lords: *Ha!*

XI
THE LAW OF THE LAND

People imagine that where an evil exists, the Queen, the
Lords and the Commons should stop it. I wonder they
have not brought in an Act of Parliament to
stop unfavourable weather on the occasion of
political demonstrations.
Robert Cecil, Marquess of Salisbury (1830–1903),
Prime Minister 1885, 1886–1892, 1895–1902

⊰ ACTS OF PARLIAMENT ⊱

Acts of Parliament begin with the words:
> *BE IT ENACTED by the Queen's most Excellent*
> *Majesty, by and with the advice and consent of the*
> *Lords Spiritual and Temporal, and Commons, in this*
> *present Parliament assembled, and by the authority of*
> *the same, as follows: –*

But **Consolidated Fund Acts** (which authorise the issue of
funds to the Government) have a preamble which says:
> *WHEREAS the Commons of the United Kingdom in*
> *Parliament assembled have resolved to authorise the*
> *use of resources and the issue of sums out of the*

Consolidated Fund to make good the supply which they have granted to Her Majesty in this Session of Parliament. Be it therefore enacted . . . .

Acts, printed on vellum: Modern record copies of the Data Protection Act 1998 and the Freedom of Information Act 2000

⊰ ANATOMY OF A BILL ⊱

Clauses (which in an Act become sections):
1. This is a clause
    (1) This is a subsection –
        (a) This is a paragraph
            (i) This is a sub-paragraph.

Schedules (which in a Bill come after all the clauses and typically expand in detail on the clauses upon which they depend):

THIS IS A SCHEDULE

1. This is a paragraph
    (1) This is a sub-paragraph –
        (a) This is a sub-sub-paragraph.

⊰ PING-PONG ⊱

To become law, the exact text of a Bill has to be agreed upon by both Houses (and to receive Royal Assent). When a Bill introduced in one House is amended by the other House, the Bill and the amendments are sent back to the first House for them to agree to. But they may disagree. Or amend the amendments. Or offer other amendments instead. And then the second House may insist on its amendments. Or amend the first House's amendments. Or offer other amendments instead. And so on . . .

This to and fro of Bills is often called **ping-pong**. When it's close to the end of a session or an election, and the Government risks losing a major Bill if it can't get agreement with the Lords, the game is more like poker than ping-pong.

Bills are carried from one House to the other by one of the Clerks at the Table, in wig and gown, with a Message saying what their House has done to the Bill. These can get pretty complicated.

At one point in the exchanges on the Prevention of Terrorism Bill in 2005 (where the Bill went back and forth seven times in a continuous sitting from 11.30am on Thursday 10 March to 8.00pm on Friday) the Commons received this Message from the Lords:

The Lords insist on certain of their Amendments to the Prevention of Terrorism Bill, to which this House has insisted on its disagreement, for which insistence they assign their Reasons; they insist on certain of the Amendments to which this House has disagreed, for which insistence they assign their Reasons; they disagree to the Amendments proposed by this House in lieu of the Lords Amendments, for which disagreement they assign their Reason; they do not insist on the remaining Amendments to which this House has disagreed; and they agree to the remaining Amendments made by this House on which this House had insisted.

Clear?

As a Bill goes back and forth, and amendments, proposals and counter-proposals are made, the master copy of the Bill is marked up with what each House has done to it, on each occasion in a different colour:

The 'House Bill' is prepared by the first House on *yellow* paper, interleaved with *green* blank pages for amendments to be added.

Second House amendments are pasted onto the interleaves and marked into the Bill in *black*.

The first House then amends in *red*.

The second House then amends in *green*.
The first House then amends in *violet*.
The second House then amends in *brown*.
The first House then amends in *blue*.
The second House then amends in *yellow*.
The first House then amends in *pink*.
The second House then amends in *cyan*.
The first House then amends in *silver*.
The second House then amends in *indigo*.
The first House then amends in *gold*.
The second House then amends in *light green*.
The first House then amends in *orange*.
The second House then amends in *dark grey*.

And if the Bill is still going to and fro after these 15 exchanges (which no Bill has yet done) the Clerks in the two Public Bill Offices will have to think of something else.

But it's not all medieval technology. Parliament uses some of the most sophisticated text handling software in the world, and while the Clerks are carrying the Bill to and fro down the corridor, across the Central Lobby and into the other House – as they have for centuries – the electronic text is put on a drive shared between the Public Bill Offices of the two Houses.

⊰ FERRET ⊱

When a Bill or a formal Message goes from one House to the other, it is tied with silk ribbon of the colour of the sending House: green for the Commons, red for the Lords. The ribbon is called *ferret* – a word long obsolete in this meaning, except at Westminster. The origin is a fine silk ribbon which originated in Florence. It was decorated with flowers – *fioretti* – hence, after several centuries, *ferret*.

⊰ AN OPTIMISTIC PREDICTION ⊱

It is rare for Acts of Parliament to have a Preamble – in other words an explanation of why the legislation is needed. The Parliament Act 1911 gave the Commons power to override the rejection of a Bill by the Lords. But in 1911 this was seen as a temporary measure:

Whereas it is expedient that provision should be made for regulating the relations between the two Houses of Parliament:

And whereas it is intended to substitute for the House of Lords as it at present exists a Second Chamber constituted on a popular instead of hereditary basis, but such substitution cannot immediately be brought into operation:

And whereas provision will require hereafter to be made by Parliament in a measure effecting such substitution for limiting and defining the powers of the new Second Chamber, but it is expedient to make such provision as in this Act appears for restricting the existing powers of the House of Lords . . .

88 years later the House of Lords Act 1999 barred all but 92 hereditary peers from sitting in the Lords; but the possibility of some or all of the members of that House being popularly elected remains a subject of bitter controversy.

⊸ ACTS REPEALED ⊱

Acts repealed by the Statute Law Repeals Act 2008 as *no longer of practical utility* included:

 The Disorderly Houses Act 1751
 The Gloucester Gaol Act 1781
 The Servants' Characters Act 1792
 The Tewkesbury Gaol Act 1813
 The Unlawful Drilling Act 1819
 The London Bread Act 1819
 The East India Company and the Nabobs of the Carnatic Act 1826

⚔ ROYAL ASSENT ⚔

All Bills, once agreed upon by the two Houses, must receive the Assent of the Sovereign (as the third element of Parliament). The Queen signs a list of Bills, rather than each one individually, and the list (or Letters Patent) is embossed with the Great Seal.

The 'Banbury Patent' raising Viscount Wallingford to be Earl of Banbury. Charles I is portrayed on the the initial 'C' of Carolus.

Notifying each House of the Bills given Royal Assent is done with little ceremony except at the Prorogation of Parliament (at the end of a session, usually in November) or at a dissolution before a general election, when the Speaker and Members of the Commons go up to the House of Lords.

On that occasion, as the title of each Bill is read by the

Clerk of the Crown in Chancery, the Clerk of the Parliaments pronounces the Royal Assent in Norman French.

For most Bills the formula is *La Reyne le veult* [The Queen wishes it], but for Bills of aids and supplies – those which authorise taxes or the granting of 'supply' (money) to the Sovereign (in effect, her Government) – the formula is *La Reyne remercie ses bons sujets, accepte leur benevolence et ainsi le veult* [thanks her good subjects, accepts their generosity and so wishes it].

Royal Assent has not been refused since 1707–1708, when Queen Anne refused her Assent to a bill for settling the militia in Scotland, using the formula *La Reyne s'avisera* [will consider what to do].

⊰ QUEEN'S CONSENT ⊱

Queen's consent is nothing to do with Royal Assent, which comes at the end of the legislative process. But when a Bill is to be introduced into either House which affects the Royal Prerogative (the things that the Monarch can do of her own authority, such as making treaties, declaring war, and a host of other things) or which affects the personal property or interests of the Crown, Queen's Consent is given for the Bill to proceed.

If the effect on the Prerogative is significant – for example, a major constitutional Bill – the fact that the Queen has given her Consent is read out by a Privy Counsellor before second reading, in these terms:

> *Her Majesty, having been informed of the purport of the Bill, has consented to place her Prerogative at the disposal of Parliament for the purposes of the Bill.*

⊰ A LETTER TO *THE TIMES* ⊱

Ramsay MacDonald, then Prime Minister, had written to Neville Chamberlain saying that *Acts of Parliament are not passed to make illegal specific acts that either you or I think are legal. They are passed to define what illegality is – i.e., a political strike.* **A.P. Herbert** (later Sir Alan Herbert, MP for the Oxford University seat) was quick to react:

Sir,

The Prime Minister, in his last letter to Mr Neville Chamberlain, has burst, somewhat unexpectedly, into humour. Perhaps, therefore, I may trespass into politics.

Is there not a simple solution to this rather childish controversy? I suggest that the Trade Disputes Bill be withdrawn and a two-clause measure be substituted, as follows:

REVOLUTION (ENABLING) BILL
1. A revolution shall be lawful if it be conducted by the manual workers in two or more basic industries.

2. It shall be lawful for the income-tax payers to combine together to refuse payment of income-tax, provided that the primary purpose of such refusal be to further a financial dispute and not to embarrass the Government.

This, unlike most modern legislation, would be not only lucid but just. I cannot hope that this measure would goad the Parliamentary Liberal Party to unanimity, but almost every other citizen would be satisfied.

I am, Sir, your obedient servant,
A. P. HERBERT
February 9th, 1931

MORE ECHOES OF THE PAST

When Bills go from one House to the other, they are 'endorsed' by the Clerk of that House with a formula in Norman French . . .

For a Bill **sent to the Lords**:
Soit baillé aux Seigneurs.

For a Lords Bill **agreed to by the Commons** (with amendments):
A ceste Bille avecque des Amendemens les Communes sont assentus.

For an **amendment made by the Lords** and agreed to by the Commons:
> *A ceste Amendement les Communes sont assentus.*

And for **most of the other traffic**, including reasons given for disagreeing to Lords Amendments:
> *Ceste Bille est remise aux Seigneurs avecque des Amendemens et des Raisons.*

◄ THE PRESSURE OF LEGISLATION ►

In 1993 Parliament passed **2,645 A4 pages** of primary legislation; in 2000, 3,841 pages; and in 2006, 4,911 pages. In 2006 there were also 11,562 pages of delegated (secondary) legislation.

◄ THE WEIGHT OF LEGISLATION ►

One of the largest Bills was the Corporation Tax Bill in session 2008–2009, which consolidated and simplified existing legislation on corporation tax. It was 819 pages long, and the interleaved copy carried up to the Lords by one of the Commons Clerks at the Table weighed 4.35 kilograms (more than 9½ pounds).

XII
CEREMONY AND COMEDY

*What I like about the [Order of the] Garter is that
there's no damn merit about it.*

Lord Melbourne

⚜ QUEEN ELIZABETH I OPENS ⚜
PARLIAMENT

This account of the Opening of Parliament on 2 April 1571 describes a ceremony entirely recognisable nearly four-and-a-half centuries later. Today the Queen arrives at the Houses of Parliament at about 11.15am and reads the Speech from the Throne at about 11.30am.

> . . . *the Queen's Highness our most gracious Sovereign, the Lady Elizabeth, about eleven of the clock, left her Palace at Whitehall. And thus she made her ancient, accustomed, most honourable passage along the road towards Westminster. First appeared Her Majesty's guard of state; and then, attended by heralds, pursuivants, and trumpeters, the ministers of justice, of religion and of government followed in solemn order, one*

after the other – knights, bannerets, esquires, judges, barons, bishops, earls, viscounts and the officers of royalty bearing the Great Seal of England, the gilt Rod of Royal State, the golden-sheathed Sword and the jewelled Cap of Maintenance, all vested in their Parliament robes, mantles, circots and hoods. Then came the Queen – the Lady Elizabeth, robed imperially, and upon her head a wreath or coronet of gold, gleaming with pearls and precious stones. Her coach was followed by the Master of the Horse, and by forty-seven Ladies and Women of Honour, a company of the Royal Beefeaters, in gold-laced coats, going on every side of them; trumpeters sounding, heralds riding, all keeping room and places orderly.

Her Majesty thus being conducted, with royalty, into the Upper House of Parliament, and apparelled in her Parliament robes, there she sat in princely and seemly sort, under a high and rich canopy; the Lords spiritual and temporal, before her, ranged in order due, and the judges on the woolsack in the midst. Notice then that the queen was on the throne was given to the knights, citizens and burgesses of the House of Commons. They, thereupon, repairing to the Parliament house, were let in and stood together behind the bar at the lower end. The queen Elizabeth then rose from her regal seat, and with a princely grace and singularly good countenance, spake a few words thus: 'My right loving Lords, and you our right faithful and obedient subjects, We, in the Name of God, and for His Service, and for the safety of this State, are now here assembled, to His glory, I hope; and

I pray that it may be to your comfort, and to our common quiet and to yours and all ours for ever.'

Sir Simonds D'Ewes (1602–1650)

⊰ QUEEN VICTORIA OPENS PARLIAMENT ⊱

From *The Illustrated London News* (16 December 1854):

On Tuesday last Her Majesty the Queen opened Parliament in person, and has inaugurated the Session in circumstances more critical and more momentous than any that have occurred since 1815. Those circumstances, however, appear to have given an impetus to the zeal and loyalty of the people, who received the Queen with a degree of enthusiasm which it would be impossible for any language to exaggerate.

The day was extremely fine, and the number of persons who showed themselves eager to catch a glimpse of the Royal procession was quite equal to that of any former occasion. All the places which afforded accommodation for that purpose were occupied at an early hour in the morning . . .

On leaving the Palace her Majesty was greeted with a true English cheer, which she courteously acknowledged. From the Palace to the Horse Guards there was a continuous line of people . . . Indeed, the crowd in the Park was so great that some danger was apprehended lest, in their eagerness to follow her

Majesty, the people might break through the Horse Guards into Whitehall and Parliament Street, where thousands had already assembled. By means of barriers, which had been erected at convenient distances from each other, the police were enabled to keep the people back, and no accidents, as far as we could learn, occurred. Her Majesty's Ministers drove rapidly along the line of route, and those of them who were recognised were cheered.

Both the Queen's Speech, and the debates in the Lords and Commons which followed, were taken up with the Crimean War.

⊰ SEARCHING THE CELLARS ⊱

The cellars under the House of Lords are searched every year before the State Opening, following the Gunpowder Plot in 1605. In November 1682 the Surveyor General of His Majesty's Works was one Sir Christopher Wren, who was enjoined:

. . . forthwith to cleer and cause to be cleered the Sellars and Vaults under and neer adjoyninge the house of Peers, Painted Chamber and Court of Requests of all Timber, firewood, coles and other materials of what kind soever and that passages be made throughout . . . that Gardes may pass throughout the Day or Night.

⚜ THE CEREMONIAL TO BE OBSERVED ⚜
AT THE OPENING OF PARLIAMENT

This is a splendid printed document signed by the Duke of Norfolk, and circulated afresh for each State Opening, which provides a minute-by-minute script for the grand occasion:

PRELIMINARY MOVEMENTS

10.30 The doors are closed to the public.

10.30 The Honourable Corps of Gentlemen at Arms assemble at the top of the Sovereign's Staircase and the Queen's Body Guard of the Yeomen of the Guard assemble in Royal Court.

10.44 A dismounted detachment of the Household Cavalry arrives at the Norman Porch and lines the Sovereign's Staircase.

10.47 The Yeomen of the Guard ascend the Sovereign's Staircase and enter the Royal Gallery.

10.52 The Gentlemen at Arms proceed to the Prince's Chamber.

10.52 The Crown, the Cap of Maintenance and the Sword of State arrive at the Sovereign's Entrance.

10.55 The Crown, the Cap of Maintenance and the Sword of State are carried under escort to the Royal Gallery.

10.58 The Officers of Arms proceed from the Prince's Chamber to the Sovereign's Staircase.

11.01 The Crown is borne by the Lord Great Chamberlain into the Robing Room.

> *11.03 The Lord Privy Seal proceeds to the top of the*
> *Sovereign's Staircase . . .*

. . . and so on.

In the final instructions, there is a delightful suggestion of informality:

> *The Gentlemen at Arms, having handed in their axes,*
> *proceed to the Norman Porch.*

Evidently current legislation on the carrying of edged weapons is a powerful discouragement to taking one's axe home.

But the instructions on the dress to be worn for the occasion are strictly formal:

DRESS (a Collar Day)

Peers: Robes over Full Dress Uniform, Morning Dress or Lounge Suit.

The Lord High Chancellor and the Lord Speaker: Full Ceremonial Dress.

The Lord Great Chamberlain, the Captain of the Honourable Corps of Gentlemen at Arms and the Captain of the Yeomen of the Guard: Full Dress Uniform without Robes.

The Master of the Horse, Gold Stick in Waiting, the Chief of the Defence Staff, the Gentleman Usher of the Black Rod, the Comptroller Lord Chamberlain's Office,

Officers of Arms, Serjeants at Arms, Equerries in Waiting, Pages of Honour, Gentlemen at Arms and Yeomen of the Guard: Full Dress Uniform.

The Lord Steward and Others: Morning Dress with which Stars of Orders limited to two in number, Decorations and Medals may be worn. Knights of the several Orders will wear their respective Collars.

NORFOLK
Earl Marshal

◄ BLACK ROD LOSES HIS WAY ►

In the early months of the Second World War it was clear that Parliament needed alternative accommodation, either in case of an increased threat from air raids, or in the event of parts of the Palace of Westminster being destroyed. Church House, the other side of Westminster Abbey from the Palace, was chosen, and on 7 November 1940, both Houses met there for the first time: the Lords in the Hall of Convocation and the Commons in the Hoare Memorial Hall. The first sitting in the Hoare Memorial Hall was recalled by Sir Henry ('Chips') Channon:

> . . . *there was noise and muffled excitement, and ministers tumbling over one another. Winston watched the confusion with amusement. The atmosphere was gay, almost like the Dorchester. Outside in the cloisters I ran*

into several clerics who seemed indignant that their building should have been taken for such lay purposes as law making.

On 21 November 1940 the King opened the new session of Parliament in Church House. Another eyewitness described the scene:

The House of Lords were sitting in a room about the size of a modest drawing-room – the doors were so narrow that the King and Queen, hand in hand as tradition dictates, were unable to enter side by side. – and fewer than 100 people were present on this historic occasion. I was fortunate enough to be one of them.

The House was far from the Commons Chamber, and the way from one to the other was winding and puzzling.

Black Rod, the Lords' official Messenger, was dispatched to 'command' the Commons to wait upon the King. Off he went and, according to custom, everywhere he appeared the police cried 'Make way for Black Rod!'. That official, new to the building, completely lost himself in the maze, and every time he approached a policeman to ask the way, he was received with a stentorian shout of 'Make way for Black Rod!' which sent him, blushing and silent, on his way.

Eventually he, by accident, found the Members' Lobby of the Commons and, with a sigh of relief, stepped forward briskly to give the traditional three hearty raps on the door, to demand admittance.

But a watchful doorkeeper leaped forward just as the heavy Rod was about to descend, and arrested the arm of the bewildered emissary of their Lordships. The Commons official silently raised a heavy curtain that covered the door – and there, right where the heavy blow would have landed, showed a pane of glass! Exactly what would have been the effect inside the silent Chamber, had Black Rod smashed the glass, can only be left to the imagination.

Guy Eden

⚔ THE KING'S CHAMPION ⚔

The King's Champion is an hereditary office held by the Dymoke family for the last 600 years. It used to be the custom to hold a great banquet in Westminster Hall on the evening of Coronation Day. The King's Champion, in full armour, would ride into the Hall and throw down a gauntlet, offering to challenge anyone who denied the King's right to succeed. This did not always go smoothly . . .

In 1685 (James II) the Champion bent to kiss the king's hand and, under the weight of full armour, keeled over and had to be lifted back onto his feet.

In 1689 (William and Mary) the gauntlet was thrown down and swiftly picked up by an old woman who disappeared into the crowd, leaving a piece of paper offering a duel in Hyde Park.

In 1764 (George II) the Champion's horse became a little confused and walked in backwards (and continued backwards all the way up the Hall to the King).

In 1821 (George IV) the Champion's horse had its head turned by the applause and went into a routine of tricks. It was said that its past had included the circus. This may have been a factor in the Dymoke family not having been asked to repeat the challenge since 1821.

⇥ LAST WORDS ⇤

Oliver Cromwell (1599–1658):
> *My design is to make what haste I can to be gone.*

Charles James Fox (1749–1806):
> *I die happy.*

William Pitt the Younger (1759–1806). Either (authorised version):
> *Oh! My country! How I love my country!*

or (unauthorised version):
> *I think I could eat one of Bellamy's veal pies.*

Spencer Perceval (1762–1812):
>   *Murder!'* (on being shot by John Bellingham in the Lobby of the House of Commons, 11 May 1812)

Lord Palmerston (1784–1865):
>   *Die, my dear Doctor? That's the last thing I shall do.*

Attributed to **William Ewart Gladstone** (1809–1898):
>   *I feel better now.*

Arthur James Balfour (1848–1930) (nearly last words):
>   *I do not think, so far as I can judge in the absence of actual experience, that I am afraid of dying.*

⊰ THE GREAT CHARTIST PETITION ⊱

The Great Chartist Petition for universal suffrage was presented to the House of Commons on 10 April 1848. It was said to have been signed by 5,706,000 people. But the Committee appointed to scrutinise public petitions found otherwise:

>   *. . . upon a careful examination . . . in which thirteen law stationers' clerks were engaged for upwards of thirteen hours, the number of signatures has been ascertained to be 1,975,496; it is further evident to your Committee that on numerous consecutive sheets the signatures are in one and the same handwriting. Your Committee have*

also observed the names of distinguished individuals attached to the Petition, who cannot be supposed to have concurred in its prayer, and as little to have subscribed to it.

Amongst such occur the names of Her Majesty, in one place as Victoria Rex., April 1st, The Duke of Wellington, KG, Sir Robert Peel, &c, &c, &c. In addition to this species of abuse, your Committee have observed another . . . namely, the insertion of names which are obviously altogether fictitious, such as 'No Cheese', 'Pug-Nose' . . . &c. There are other words and phrases which, though written in the form of signatures . . . your Committee will not hazard offending the House . . . by reporting, though it may be added, that they are obviously signatures belonging to no human being.

⊰ POLITICAL REALISM ⊱

I saw an old man in the park.
I asked the old man why
He watched the couples after dark
And he gave this strange reply:

I am the Royal Commission on Kissing,
Appointed by Gladstone in '74.
Most of my colleagues are dead or missing.

Our minutes were lost in the last Great War.
But still I'm a Royal Commission.
Our task I intend to see through.
Though I know as an old politician
Not a thing will be done if I do.

A.P. Herbert, 'Pageant of Parliament', in *Mild and Bitter* (1936)

⊰ POLITICS ⊱

Alan Clark:
There are no true friends in politics. We are all sharks circling, and waiting for traces of blood to appear in the water.

Peter Ustinov:
I could never have been a politician. I couldn't bear to be right all the time.

Lord Randolph Churchill:
I have tried all forms of excitement, from tip-cat to tiger-shooting; all degrees of gambling, from beggar-my-neighbour to Monte Carlo; but have found no gambling like politics, and no excitement like a big division in the House of Commons.

⚔ MINISTERIAL RED BOXES ⚖

These boxes are a combination of briefcase, in-tray and status symbol; they cost about £700 each.

⚔ GRAFFITI ⚖

Guy Fawkes was the sanest man who ever went into Parliament . . . and look what happened to him.

Lord Denning rules – OK!
House of Lords overrules – OK!

In debate on the Education Bill in 1870, one criticism was that it might lead to more graffiti . . . only *lower down.*

⚔ COMPETITIVE EXAMINATION ⚖

Until 1887 there was no examination for entry to a Clerkship in the House of Commons – indeed, no qualification was required other than that of being well looked upon as a candidate by the Clerk of the House of Commons himself. But in 1886 the Clerk of the House, Sir Reginald Palgrave, declared his *intention, whilst responsible for the appointment of*

*the Clerks to the Department of the Clerk of the House of
Commons, to make such appointments turn on the result of a
competitive examination among such candidates as I may
nominate for that purpose ... The competitors for each vacancy
... shall range between three and six in number.*

This was more than 30 years after the Northcote-Trevelyan
Report of 1854, which led to the establishment of a Civil
Service recruited openly and on merit. Although Clerks
were (and are) emphatically not civil servants, Palgrave
may have thought that he needed to move with the times.
But cautiously ... the candidates would have an exam, but
he would choose who should be the candidates.

SCHEDULE OF EXAMINATION

Obligatory

1. Handwriting and orthography.
2. The power of accurate comparison of a copy
   with the original document.
3. Arithmetic, including vulgar and decimal
   fractions.
4. English composition.
5. History of England, from AD 1603 to the year
   1860.
6. Constitutional History of England. Books to
   be read: – Hallam and May's Constitutional
   Histories; Dicey on the Law of the
   Constitution; Anson on the Law and Custom
   of the Constitution.
7. Latin: The qualifying test is from Latin into

English; but marks will be given in the competition for translation from English into Latin.

Optional

8. Greek: Translation from Greek into English, and from English into Greek.
9. Elementary mathematics.
10. French.
11. German.

Every candidate must show a competent knowledge of the obligatory subjects, and may select any two of the optional subjects.

Limits of age, 19 to 25.

Those between 19 and 24, whose parents do not reside in London or the vicinity, must be provided with such a place of residence as shall meet with the approval of the Clerk of the House of Commons.

⊰ GWYNETH DUNWOODY (1930–2008) ⊱

Gwyneth Dunwoody was the Member for Exeter 1966–1970, and for Crewe and Nantwich 1974–2008; a classic modern example of an independent-minded MP.

Self-description: *Awkward old bat.*

I don't mind being called a battle-axe; they are usually well-made, very sharp and very good at doing their job.

Of her dress sense: *I'm not employed for my dress sense.*

Of Parliament: *For me, Parliament is not only the last important forum for the British people, it is also the last defender of the rights of all citizens.*

⚜ ADVICE TO NEW MEMBERS ⚜

From **Clement Attlee**: *Specialise. And stay out of the bars.*

⚜ TO AN INEFFICIENT MEMBER ⚜
OF A SELECT COMMITTEE

A letter from **Oliver Cromwell**:
> *To Mr Waters, at the Cross Keys: these in all speed.*
>
> *Sir,*
> *If no more be done than you and yours have done, it is well you give over such powers as you have to those*

who will. I say to you now my mind thereto: If I have not that aid which is my due, I say to you I will take it. And so heed me; for I find your words are mere wind: I shall do as I say, if I find no aid come to me by Tuesday.

Sir, I rest, as you will,
OLIVER CROMWELL

On 3 September 1969, the 311th anniversary of Cromwell's death, *The Times* carried two announcements next to each other in its 'In Memoriam' column:

OLIVER CROMWELL, 25th April 1599–3rd September 1658. Lord Protector, 1653–1658. Statesman, General and Ruler. Let God arise, let His enemies be scattered – Psalm 68 verse 1.

CROMWELL – To the eternal condemnation of Oliver, Seditionist, Traitor, Regicide, Racialist, proto-Fascist and blasphemous Bigot. God save England from his like.

⊰ YET MORE OLD CHESTNUTS ⊱

After a run of all-night sittings an MP's wife stopped believing that her husband was engaged on parliamentary duties. He returned at 3.30am after a series of votes on the report stage of the Criminal Justice (Miscellaneous Provisions) (Scotland) Bill to find a note which said:

> *The day before yesterday you came home yesterday morning. Yesterday you came home this morning. So if today you come home tomorrow morning you will find that I left you yesterday.*

An eager young MP, addressing constituency audience which has had enough of politics: *Can you all hear me? Can you hear me at the back?*

Weary voice from the back: *Yes, I can hear you. But I don't mind swapping with somebody who can't.*

An equally eager new MP, told by a cash-strapped TV producer who can't pay much of a fee to the participants on his discussion programme: *I'm afraid it's . . . well . . . it's £50.*

Eager new MP: *Right! Will you take a cheque or would cash be easier?*

A bibulous 19th-century peer slightly the worse for wear, encounters an acquaintance and admits to having drunk three bottles of port the previous evening. *Good Heavens, my Lord*, says the acquaintance. *Three bottles without assistance! Not quite*, replies his Lordship, *I had the assistance of a bottle of Madeira.*

Ernest Bevin, on hearing a fellow MP remark that Nye Bevan was his own worst enemy: *Not while I'm around, he's not.*

(This is included in chestnuts because, while many confidently tell it of Bevin and Bevan, there are as many who tell it of any number of sworn enemies.)

A female constituent of somewhat nervous disposition comes to see her MP at the House. She sends in a 'green card' seeking an interview, and waits in the Central Lobby. A few minutes later there is a vote in the Commons. Bells ring, people run about, and there is a deafening shout of *DEEEEVISION* from the policemen. The old lady is much alarmed, and plucks up courage to ask one of the policemen: *Please can you tell me what's happening? Well, to tell you the truth, mum*, says the constable, *one of 'em's got out.*

A dutiful constituency MP, constantly busy with opening fêtes, attending sports days and generally putting himself about, begins to notice a female constituent at most of these events. She is, shall we say, not good-looking, and somehow always manages to catch his eye and nod and smile. One day she comes up to him and thrusts an envelope into his hand. He puts it into his pocket and later gives it to his super-efficient secretary with a bundle of other constituency post.

Back at his desk at Westminster the letters for his personal attention are laid out on his desk. On top is the one from the female constituent. It says how much she admires all he does for the constituency, and asks, as a special favour, for a signed photograph. It is signed with her name followed by 'Horseface' in brackets. The MP thinks, well, she *is* pretty ugly, but how splendid to come to terms with it and adopt this as a pet name. Suppressing the feeling that he is being stalked, the MP also reflects that she is obviously a firm supporter, and that one upsets people like that at one's peril.

So he takes out a photograph of the largest size, signs it *With best wishes to dear Horseface,* puts it in a frame (nothing too good for such a loyal supporter), puts the whole thing in a padded bag and drops it in the post.

The next morning his secretary comes in and he recounts his good deed of yesterday. *Well done,* says the secretary, *I was afraid that you wouldn't remember which one she was just from the name, so I put 'Horseface' in brackets after the signature.*

Ernest Bevin: *My policy is to be able to buy a ticket at Victoria Station and go anywhere I damn well please.*

Winston Churchill: *Men occasionally stumble over the truth, but pick themselves up and hurry off as if nothing had happened.*

Harold Wilson: *Every time Mr Macmillan comes back from abroad, Mr Butler goes to the airport and grips him warmly by the throat.*

Sir Barnett Cocks, Clerk of the House of Commons 1962–1973: *A committee is a cul-de-sac down which ideas are lured and then quietly strangled.*

Sir Geoffrey Howe: *The post of Leader of the House of Commons . . . is all too often used as some kind of Cabinet departure lounge.*

Francis Pym: *A large majority is a very dangerous thing.*

◄ WHEN MICHAEL FOOT ►

When Michael Foot as Leader of the Labour Party went to Brussels to chair a group seeking unilateral disarmament as part of the Labour Party's policy for the European Parliament elections he made a headline writer's dreams come true:
FOOT HEADS ARMS BODY

◄ WALDER'S LAW ►

Walder's Law was stated by David Walder, MP for High Peak 1961–1966 and then Clitheroe from 1970 until his death in 1978, and a witty novelist. Walder's Law is:
The first three people to speak at a meeting of the 1922 Committee [the backbench committee of the Conservative Party], *on any subject whatsoever, are mad.*

⚜ THE BUDGET ⚜

The Budget is the Chancellor of the Exchequer's annual review of the nation's finances and proposals for taxation for the following year and is normally delivered in March or April (although from 1993 to 1996 Kenneth Clarke's Budgets were combined with a statement on spending plans and were delivered in November).

The term 'budget' comes from the French *bougette*, a little bag. 'To open your budget' came to mean 'to speak your mind frankly'.

The Budget box held up by the Chancellor outside Number 11 Downing Street before he sets off for the House of Commons used to be the battered red despatch box used by Gladstone in the 1860s, and by every Chancellor (except James Callaghan) since then. From 1997 the new Chancellor, Gordon Brown, used a despatch box made for him by trainees in his constituency. His successor Alastair Darling went back to the battered old box.

The longest continuous Budget speech was delivered by Gladstone in 1853. It lasted four hours and 45 minutes. Disraeli's speech the previous year lasted a total of five hours, but with a break.

The shortest Budget speech was Disraeli's in 1867: just 45 minutes. In recent years budget speeches have been about an hour. Gordon Brown's 2007 speech was his shortest at

51 minutes; his 2000 and 2005 speeches each lasted 52 minutes, as did both of Alastair Darling's Budget speeches, in 2008 and 2009.

The most Budget speeches were made by Gladstone (12), followed by Brown (11) and Lloyd George (7). One Chancellor never made a Budget speech: Iain Macleod became Chancellor after the Conservatives' June 1970 election victory, but died on 20 July 1970.

Refreshing the economy . . . Chancellors have over the years felt the need for greater sustenance than the carafe of water on the Table of the House can provide. Kenneth Clarke had a modest glass of whisky at his side; Geoffrey Howe, gin and tonic; Nigel Lawson, a spritzer; Benjamin Disraeli, brandy and water; and William Gladstone, sherry with an egg beaten up in it. Lloyd George's voice was restored by warm beef tea during a half-hour break two hours and 47 minutes into his 1909 Budget speech. He returned and spoke for a further hour and 47 minutes.

Nothing in the till! said by **Winston Churchill** (last Budget, April 1929), arms flung wide, to Philip Snowden (first Budget, April 1930), as the two met on the steps of the Treasury. Many think it significant that the statue of Churchill in Parliament Square looks towards the House of Commons . . . but has its back to the Treasury.

Budget secrecy is always intense, not least because of the market sensitivity of much of its contents. In 1936, Jimmy

Thomas, a Cabinet Minister, was found to have leaked Budget proposals to a Conservative MP. He resigned from the Government and then, shortly afterwards, from the House. In 1947 Hugh Dalton, on his way to the Chamber to deliver his Budget speech, spoke casually to a lobby journalist about its contents – perhaps thinking that it mattered less when there was apparently no time to make use of the information. But the news was in the *Star* before Dalton left the Chamber. He apologised to the House and resigned. In 1996 Kenneth Clarke's final Budget was leaked almost in its entirety to the *Daily Mirror*. But the paper refused to use it, and handed the papers back to the Treasury.

Sir Geoffrey Howe, Chancellor of the Exchequer 1979–1983, had a dog called Budget.

John Major's Budget speech in 1990 was the **first Budget speech to be televised**.

Income tax was introduced in 1799 as a 'temporary' measure to help finance the Napoleonic wars. In the debate on Pitt's Budget of 3 December 1798 a Member said:

> *An excise man comes to a man's dwelling to see whether he has taken into or sent out of his house some particular articles without paying a given sum to the Revenue; but here [with income tax] a spy comes not only into the house but opens the bureau of every man and becomes acquainted with his most secret concerns.*

A man must show to this spy his bills, his notes, his bonds and all his securities. This is monstrous.

When **Henry Addington** as Prime Minister and Chancellor of the Exchequer proposed the abolition of income tax in 1802, he told the House of Commons:

This burden should not be left to rest on the shoulders of the public in time of peace because it should be reserved for the important occasions which, I trust, will not soon recur.

The Budget 1791:

Receipts	£16,030,286.0s.0d.	[2009 equivalent: £898,176,246]
Expenditure	£15,969,178.0s.0d.	[2009 equivalent: £894,753,043]
Balance	£61,108.0s.0d.	[2009 equivalent: £3,423,203]

The *Journal* (10 May 1791)

The Budget 2009:

Receipts	£496,000,000,000
Expenditure	£671,000,000,000
Balance	-£175,000,000,000

Financial Statement and Budget Report (April 2009)

EPILOGUE

⚜ PRAYERS FOR THE PARLIAMENT ⚜

Every sitting of the House of Commons begins with prayers, read by the Speaker's Chaplain, and lasting about three minutes. The public are not admitted to prayers, and they are not televised. In the Lords, the prayers are read by the Bishops who are Members of that House, taking it in turns to do so day by day.

After Psalm 67 (*God be merciful to us and bless us*) and the Lord's Prayer, the prayers for the Parliament are:

O Lord our heavenly Father, high and mighty, King of kings, Lord of lords, the only Ruler of princes, who dost from thy throne behold all the dwellers on the earth; most heartily we beseech thee with thy favour to behold our most Gracious Sovereign Lady Queen Elizabeth, and so replenish her with the grace of thy Holy Spirit, that she may always incline to thy will, and walk in thy way: endue her plenteously with heavenly gifts, grant her long to live, strengthen her that she may vanquish and overcome all her enemies; and finally after this life she may attain everlasting joy and felicity, through Jesus Christ our Lord. Amen.

Lord, the God of righteousness and truth, grant to our Queen and her government, to members of Parliament and all in positions of responsibility, the guidance of your Spirit. May they never lead the nation wrongly through love of power, desire to please, or unworthy ideals; but laying aside all private interests and prejudices keep in mind their responsibility to seek to improve the condition of all mankind; so may your kingdom come and your name be hallowed.

Amen.